I0023163

PRESENT FORCES IN NEGRO PROGRESS

W. D. WEATHERFORD, Ph.D.

ISBN: 978-1-63923-857-6

All Rights reserved. No part of this book maybe reproduced without written permission from the publishers, except by a reviewer who may quote brief passages in a review to be printed in a newspaper or magazine.

Printed: March 2023

Published and Distributed By:
Lushena Books
607 Country Club Drive, Unit E
Bensenville, IL 60106
www.lushenabks.com

ISBN: 978-1-63923-857-6

Dedicated to that growing company of interested Southern white men and to that group of sympathetic men in the North, whose united interest in the Negro Race is a prophecy of a better day.

253811

ON BEING BROUGHT FROM AFRICA TO AMERICA

'Twas mercy brought me from my pagan land,
Taught my benighted soul to understand
That there's a God—that there's a Saviour too;
Once I redemption neither sought nor knew.
Some view our sable race with scornful eye—
"Their color is a diabolic dye."
Remember, Christians, Negroes black as Cain
May be refined, and join the angelic train.

—*Phillis Wheatley.*

CONTENTS

PREFACE

In venturing on this second volume concerning the much vexed question of race relationships, I can only ask the same cordial response which the former effort elicited. When "Negro Life in the South" was sent out to the college men of the country, it was with the greatest misgivings. I am persuaded that not the merit of the book but the overmastering importance of the subject has called forth a response far beyond expectation. Already, more than ten thousand college men in the South have used this little volume in the study groups of the college Young Men's Christian Associations. Many of these groups have asked for a further study of this subject, and it is in response to this call that the present volume is sent forth.

I am greatly indebted to the large number of students and professors, in white and colored schools alike, who have helped in gathering the material for this undertaking. Also, I must express my appreciation to the farm demonstrators in the South, superintendents of education and hosts of others who have so fully and cordially responded to my requests for facts.

As in the former volume, I have attempted to be fair to all concerned. *The supreme need of the hour is that men shall face facts rather than spin theories.* No sane or fair-minded man can excuse his own ignorance of so important a subject. My effort, therefore, has been to state conditions as they are, even though such statements at times have seemed harsh. I confidently believe that all well-wishers of the race will be glad to face these facts in the same spirit of fairness. Perhaps it may be important to say, as in the preface to the former volume, that the author is a Southern man, educated in the South, and now living and working in that section, where he has a chance to know the Negro as he is.   W. D. WEATHERFORD.

Nashville, Tennessee,
    May 1, 1912.

CHAPTER I

TRAITS OF NEGRO CHARACTER

CHAPTER I

TRAITS OF NEGRO CHARACTER

PAUL, the seclusive Jew, but also the Roman citizen and world traveler, long schooled in the thought and spirit of Jesus Christ, said boldly to the proud Athenians who thronged him on the Areopagus, "God has made of one [blood] every nation of men for to dwell on the face of the earth." The dictate of deep religious conviction has settled down into the firm *postulate of modern anthropology*. Darwin's "Origin of Species" holds that all forms of life are descended from a comparatively few simple types, and that nature by a process of selection of the fittest has brought out of the variations of individuals a series of species fitted to live in the environment in which they find themselves. Whatever the original type of man was—this we are not here interested to discuss—modern anthropologists are agreed that the human family is sprung from a common origin, and hence all men are by nature akin. The differences in races are due to a long selective process extending over thousands of years, by which those characteristics of individuals, which best fitted them to the environment in which they lived, become more and more accentuated, through the dying out of all those individuals who did not possess such characteristics.

It is a commonplace fact that no two individuals are alike, and this was no less true in the dawn of the human race than it is now. Each individual had certain differentiae that set him off from all others. Anthropologists believe that as centuries passed by and as men moved out into different environments, those men possessing certain of the more prominent differentiae were able to survive; hence these differentiae combined, owing, doubtless, among other things, to climate and food supply, to set apart one group as a definite type or race. Other specific attributes surviving and becoming more prominent in a different environment combined to set apart another group; and, so it happened for as many distinct races as were able to establish themselves strongly. Among these original types, most scholars believe that the white man of Europe, the yellow man of Asia and the black man of Africa held the prevailing places. Later the mixing of these groups possessing the stronger characteristics would give rise to secondary racial types.

Races Fitted for Their Environment.

If the origin of race characteristics is such as these scientists believe it to be, then one can readily understand why the Chinese are better able to survive under Asiatic conditions than are other races; or the black man better able to survive in Africa than the white man; for through a long selective process, nature has picked out a race of men in each case whose differentiae have best fitted them to survive under specific conditions. Viewed from this standpoint, the yellow man is the fittest for Asia, *the black man is the fittest for Africa,* and the white man for certain other parts of the earth. Either of these may prove less fit for the environment of another section. But unfitness does not necessarily mean inferiority. A white man may be far less fitted for Africa than the black man, but the former is not necessarily inferior, and *vice versa.* Fitness does not consist in intellectual ability alone, but in all those qualities which combine to meet the environment at the point of highest efficiency.

Environment of the Negro.

The Negro race is that part of the human family which found its development and formed its differentiating characteristics in the tropical sections of the globe. Therefore we should expect that physically and mentally he would be so constituted as best to survive under tropical conditions. It is simply impossible to understand the Negro without taking this fact into account. Unfortunately, the white man has usually measured the Negro by his own standards, and wherein there is lack of conformity, it has been put down to the discredit of the Negro. This may or may not be a fair judgment in any particular instance. The one important thing is that we, as white men, shall come to understand sympathetically what the Negro really is, and why he is and what he is. When one goes down into the slums and sees the conditions into which children are born, he at once has a new understanding and a new sympathy for the different standards of those children. We are perfectly aware that this early environment is very apt to color the whole life of the man. Likewise when one looks into the tropical conditions where a great race was conceived by nature and born and nurtured for thousands of years, one will see how that environment has been inwrought into the very fiber of the being of that race. This will make clear the basis of those characteristics of the American Negro wherein he differs from the white man.

Frankness Needed.

In a discussion of this kind everything is to be gained by a frank statement and nothing is to be lost. It is far more important to face the facts than to make a case either for or against the Negro race. The worst must be boldly stated, the best must be gladly seen. The first will be humiliating to the best Negroes and their friends, the latter will be discomforting to the demagogue who berates the whole race.

But I am persuaded that the best white men and the best Negroes are more than eager to see conditions just as they are. I, therefore, make bold to set forth simply, but I hope clearly, the mental and moral traits of the Negro which have a practical bearing on the relationship of the two races in the South. It is to be noted, of course, that the white man possesses many or all of these characteristics in greater or less degree, for both whites and blacks started with the same general nature; but the environment of Africa has accentuated certain characteristics for the negro, and the environment of Europe has accentuated others for the whites. Therefore, we are not attempting to point out those characteristics which set him off completely from all other races, but we are trying to make a brief inventory of his weaknesses and his strength. First, let us face frankly some of his outstanding weaknesses. To the negro race these should be a challenge to improvement, for, as John Fiske, speaking from a scientific standpoint, has so well said: "The most essential feature of man is his improvableness," and with this quality no race or individual can be hopeless. On the other hand, to the white man these darker facts should be a challenge to sympathetic helpfulness.

Lack of Self-Control.

Perhaps the characteristic in which the Negro differs most radically from the white man is in lack of self-control. By this we do not mean to say that the white race, or any individual in it, has perfect self-control. No man who has half tried to live a decent life has failed to observe his weakness in this regard. Nor does it mean that there are no Negroes who have a high degree of poise and self-mastery. We mean simply that the Negro, as a race, has not so far developed what the psychologists call the power of inhibition. He cannot forego the pleasure of present gratification in order that he may reap an increased, but a far-off, reward. To him the future has little meaning. While he has an extravagant imagination, it has too little power of synthesis to be able to relate properly the facts of self-denial and future reward so that the latter becomes a living reality. In other words, he is much like the child who has not yet learned to center attention on any one thing long enough to create an abiding interest sufficiently strong to overcome the pressing interest of the immediate hour. Viewed from this standpoint, education is simply the training of the child in the art of such continued attention as will enable it to give a proper valuation to far, as well as to near events. Likewise, the progress of civilization is just the growth of the cruder types of men into the ability to restrain their present desires or appetites for the sake of a larger future good, either for themselves or for the community.

Explanation of This Lack of Self-Control.

Some reasons for this lack of self-control are not far to seek, when one looks into tropical environment. One of its commonest manifestations is what we, in common parlance, call laziness. The future reward is not vivid enough to induce a man to lay aside his present ease that he may attain a larger good in the future. This habit of self-indulgence would be greatly accentuated in a tropical climate, where the abundant hand of nature supplies most of the actual necessities of food and clothing. Furthermore, in such a climate hard labor frequently is punished by death. Those who are over-industrious are eliminated, and there is bred by natural selection a race of listless people. Work in order that one may live, is a great teacher of self-control. If a great preacher could speak with perfect propriety and good effect on the commonplace subject, "Blessed Be Drudgery" in our time, and in the midst of the most energetic and cultured type of American people, it is no wonder that a people where drudgery is unnecessary, and next to impossible should fail to develop those powers of inhibition which routine work is so well calculated to foster. Not to have to work is a handicap to any individual. But for a race to be freed from this necessity, through multiplied centuries, is to place upon the powers of decision and self-control a test which unfits them for a more strenuous environment until their nature has had time to adjust itself to the new conditions. This process must, of necessity, be slow.

Indulgence.

Furthermore, the abundance of food at one season and its paucity at another—which must inevitably be the case where there is little harvesting, but complete dependence on nature—will of itself foster a disposition to gorge during the time of plenty in order not to suffer in the leaner days. But here again is a form of indulgence which breaks down the power of self-control. This fact is believed by some to explain, in part at least, the exaggerated appetite of a great many Negroes, not only for food, but for liquors and tobacco.

Sexual Indulgence.

Then again, it is not inconceivable—and many students of social questions believe it to be a fact—that the high death rate of the tropics has put a premium on, if it has not made a necessity of a high birth rate, thus leading the native again into a form of indulgence which seems nothing less than terrible. This statement ought to lead us to admire the splendid victory of that growing company of colored people who have overcome in this fight; it ought also to make us redouble our sympathetic help for those still in the struggle.

Professor Dowd's Summary.

Speaking of this lack of inhibition among the Negroes

of the Banana Zone, from which many of the slaves came
to America, Professor Dowd says:[1]

"Their wills are inundated and paralyzed by the surging
of every passion and impulse towards immediate gratification. The riotous clamor of their passions explains their
ungovernable temper, propensity to murder, steal, lie, de-
ceive, or to overindulge their sexual appetite, their love for
liquor, tobacco or anything that may momentarily strike
their fancy. It is this same lack of restraint among civilized
people that fills their world with tragedy, strews the path
of history with blood, makes necessary wars, armies, navies,
police, jails, reformatories and hospitals and orphanages.
As a consequence of the thraldom of the Negroes to their
passions, they have become afflicted with a kind of abulia,
i. e., a certain antipathy to whatever exacts resolution, con-
straint or mental effort."

Change, A Slow Process.

These characteristics have worked themselves into the
fiber of the Negro race through long centuries of time, and
their elimination will not be the work of a day. The situation is by no means hopeless, however, for study of the
American and African negro types leads one to the delib-
erate conclusion that the American Negro is far more removed from the degradation of the mass of population in
tropical Africa than the average American white man is
removed from the ignorant American Negro. All of this
progress has been made in two or three centuries. Much of
it in one century, which is as a watch in the night compared with the centuries during which these propensities
were built up.

Restraint Needed.

What the Negro needs is encouragement to self-control.

---

[1]"The Negro Races," p. 383.

Just as the child in the home is unable to control himself and needs the fostering care of the parent, so the mass of Negroes needs the encouragement of a stronger race. As a simple illustration: if I were not in favor of prohibition for any other reason, I would be its strong advocate in the South, in order that this temptation might be removed from the path of a race of little self-mastery. It is a well-known fact that intoxicants of any kind deaden the powers of self-control, and when taken by those whose inhibitory powers are already weak, they can have no other effect than the most disastrous. I wish to mention this matter in a later chapter, but here I cannot refrain from saying that no white man who knows the far-African heredity of the Negro can honestly damn him for his self-indulgence, and still leave before him the temptation to get that which robs him of what little self-control he has been able to acquire during these brief centuries. Hon. Seaborn Wright, of Atlanta, expresses the conviction of Southern men who have honestly studied this question, and who really care, when he says, "The development, the safety, aye! the very life of the Negro race in the South hangs upon his absolute separation from intoxicating liquors."[1]

Superstition.

The next weakness of negro character which stands out prominently is superstition. Every primitive race has much of this characteristic, and indeed few if any of the most advanced races are entirely free from its power. Thus we are not discussing a characteristic which inheres in the Negro alone; we are simply trying to get a real view of the negro nature as we now find it in the South. It is unnecessary here more than to refer to the dark superstition of practically all of the African tribes. They live in constant fear of angry spirits, of the power of the fetich, of the

[1] "Social Welfare and the Liquor Problem," p. 233.

witch doctor and what not. Much of this has become so deeply ingrained in the nature of the Negro that the slaves and their descendants have never been able to shake themselves free from its terrible hold.

This superstitious fear makes almost every Negro an intense conservative, hard to move out of the old beaten way of doing things. To change means the past was wrong, and that cannot be, because providence has prospered it. A brief look, however, at some of the fields and homes would make one very loath to charge providence with any such crimes. Perhaps there is no more unprogressive or immovable mass of humanity to be found than a group of superstitious Negroes. There is no greater bar to the Negro's advancement than this fear, and the hope of the race lies in his getting a new message of life that is not based on superstitious fears of ghosts, spirits and future punishment.

Cruelty.

In view of the Negro's kindliness and good nature, it seems a strange charge to say that he is cruel to animals and dependents. Yet candor forces one to admit that this is frequently the case. Some of the horrible practices of punishment in Africa would be unbelievable did not one have the thought of the Inquisition, St. Bartholomew, the French Revolution, ever staring him in the face. Not infrequently have I seen an ignorant Negro beat his mule or horse, seemingly for the pure joy of seeing the animal wince.

In an investigation made by Mr. Stephenson, of North Carolina, concerning jury service of Negroes, it came out rather clearly that most negro defendants preferred not to have other Negroes on the Jury, because they feared cruel treatment and severity from such jurors. Whether this is so or not, almost every lawyer and judge questioned gave this as his conclusion. Dr. Odum, in his discussion of "The Social and Mental Traits of the Negro," gives more emphasis to the cruelty of the Negro than we are disposed to accept. But perhaps he is partly right when he says:[1] "And Negroes often impose severe punishments when the feeling of authority and power is given full sway. His judgments are both careless and without compassion when they are once directed against a subordinate."

Undoubtedly this cruelty is a survival of the old savagery, where the hand of every man was set against his neighbor, and so, perhaps we ought not to judge too harshly those who are separated from this ancestry by so brief a period of time. We have before remarked concerning the lack of synthetic imagination on the part of the African native. This may account to some extent for his cruelty because he is not able to put himself in the other man's place. John Fiske has put this clearly as follows:[2]

"If now we contrast the civilized man intellectually and morally with the savage, we find that, along with his vast increase of cerebral surface, he has an immensely greater power of representing in imagination objects and relations not present to the senses. This is the fundamental intellectual difference between civilized men and savages. The power of imagination, or ideal representation, underlies the whole of science and art, and it is closely connected with the ability to work hard and submit to present discomfort for the sake of a distant reward. It is also closely connected with the development of the sympathetic feelings. The better we can imagine objects and relations not present to sense, the more readily we can sympathize with other people. Half the basis of cruelty in the world is the direct result of stupid incapacity to put one's self in the other man's place."

Let us hope that better trained imaginations and a more genuine religion will help to eradicate this ugly element.

---

[1] "The Social and Mental Traits of the Negro," p. 209.
[2] "The Destiny of Man," p. 99.

Vanity and Conceit.

It is an undoubted fact that the mass of Negroes in the South are near enough to the child stage to be eager for attention and easily filled with conceit. Referring to this characteristic among African tribes of the Banana Zone, Professor Dowd says:[1] "The Negro seeks to win the applause of his fellows, usually by a gaudy exhibition of dress, trinkets or boastful language. The least word of praise or flattery gives him a lively sense of pleasure, and this soft spot in his character is one of which the shrewd white man soon learns to take advantage."

Indeed, one of the strongest objections brought against educating the Negro is the fact that it makes of him a "smart-Alec." One is forced to confess that gaudy ties, pointed shoes of extreme style, "loud" hosiery, and hats tilted to one side frequently mark the negro student who has just started. It is a pity that such should be so. But candor forces us to remember that the Negro has no monopoly on "smart-Alecdom." It is just a little more prominent and vulgar in its negro manifestation.

> "When I see a lad with his pants rolled up
> And his beautiful sox on view,
> With his red neck-tie, and his little round hat,
> With a band of marble blue,
> With his sixteen rings and his fourteen pins
> That he got at his dear prep-school,
> Why it strikes a chord and I say, "Oh, Lord!
> Was I ever that big a fool?"

And that was written of the white freshman.

Tendency to Wordiness.

Of the Negro's tendency to wordiness I know no better example than the book, "The American Negro," written by a Negro as an arraignment of the race. After charging the Negro with vanity, pomposity and conceit, he passes on to a

---

[1]"The Negro Races," p. 395.

criticism of the religious and social life of the Negro as follows:[1] "The social side of the negro life has been to me an open page of execrable weakness, of unblushing shame, of inconceivable mendacity, of indurated folly and ephemeral contrition." By this sentence alone he would prove how near he is to his African ancestor who loves nothing so well as a high-sounding palaver.

The Negro is naturally vain, conceited, verbose, pompous—every one of which traits appears in the characters created by Dunbar, himself a Negro who presumably knew them well. But real training is a splendid cure, and I am glad to say that I do not know a single well-trained Negro who allows himself to fall into these childish habits.

Lacking in Power of Initiative.

Perhaps the most fundamental weakness is the seeming lack of initiative. The Negro is a good follower. He imitates easily and accurately, but he does not seem, so far at least, to have developed much power of originality save in a few instances. The weakness of the Liberian government; the fact that there have never been any great empires built up in Africa; the failure of the churches in America to unite on any strong, aggressive policy; the absence of community life and spirit—all are indications of lack of originative and initiative ability. Of course, there are a few real leaders, like Dr. Booker T. Washington, Major R. R. Moton, of Hampton, Dr. C. T. Walker, of Augusta, Ga., and T. C. Walker, of Gloster County, Virginia, not to mention many others who have proved themselves genuine leaders of men. Perhaps as years go by and as more and more responsibility for the welfare of his race is thrown on the Negro, increasing numbers of men will be found able to respond to the call for leaders with power of initiative.

---

[1]"The American Negro," p. xxi.

Picture Not All Dark.

This is an ugly, but not altogether dark picture. In every phase of weakness here presented the American Negro is—if we may believe the records of African travelers—many stages advanced over his African ancestry. Progress has been slow, to be sure, but the start is always slow. Now that the start is well made, I confidently look to see more advancement in the next twenty-five years than we have seen in all the years since the landing of the first slaves in 1619. If the things I have said have seemed harsh, they have been said with no desire to wound, but with the one sincere purpose that white and colored alike may see the weaknesses of the Negro and unite in an effort to save him from himself. Emerson once said the purpose of a friend is to make us do what we can, and no man is a real friend to an individual or to a race who is not honest enough to see, and courageous enough to set forth the plain weaknesses found therein.

Strong Points in Negro Character.

One is glad to have said the worst in order that he may feel free to say the best without being accused of prejudice or of a one-sided view. That there are many noble traits of character in the Negro cannot for a moment be doubted by those who have taken time to think systematically through their experiences with him. Of course many of these virtues are almost lacking in many of the vagrant servant class who work only enough to keep soul and body together, but this same thing is true of the shiftless class of whites. In fact, if I must deal with a shiftless man, I believe I would take my chances on a trifling Negro rather than a trifling white man. Not a few of the managers and owners of large plantations have expressed to me this same preference.

Fidelity.

Of all the stories of faithful devotion, few read more like a romance than the simple facts of the love of the slave for his master. For years I have had an attentive ear to such stories, whether told by some white-haired old Negro who still lives in the past or by some of the old slave owners, who love to recount the gratitude and faithfulness of their slaves. Just the other day a prominent negro leader told me the simple story of his father, going to war as the body-servant of his young master, watching him in his tent, burying him when killed, and walking two hundred miles after the battle to carry back to his young mistress the gold watch and the money of her dead husband. Joel Chandler Harris and Thomas Nelson Page have made this characteristic of the Negro stand out clearly by the beauty of their plantation stories. Paul Laurence Dunbar, himself a pure blood Negro, has given the same characteristic beautiful expression in his stories, "The Staunton Coachman," "Cahoots," etc., and in such poems as "The Deserted Plantation" and "Christmas on the Plantation."

During all the dark days of the Civil War there were very few instances where Negroes deliberately betrayed a specific trust. "That was the old-time darky," many are fond of saying, but it was the Negro, for old time or new time, the essential nature of a race cannot be changed in a generation. If the "old-time negro" had in him the essential quality of fidelity to a trust, then the new Negro has that same fundamental quality, if we will only find some way to develop it. Those who talk about the angelic qualities of the "old-time darky" (I do not like the term), and damn with every breath the new Negro, simply prove their shallow thinking. They ought to know that a race characteristic cannot be developed in two or three generations unless its essential elements are there at the beginning. If fidelity was a mark of the former slave, fidelity is still a trait, though

undeveloped, in the Negro of today. We alone are responsible if we do not find means of bringing it to the surface.
Besides, it may fairly be said that few Negroes today deliberately disregard a definite charge. They may lie or steal
in petty ways, but even the poorest type of Negro rarely
betrays a specific trust.

Gratitude.

It often has been said of late years that the Negro has
no sense of gratitude. This is not in accordance with my
experience. I do not mean to say that I have not done
things for Negroes where the latter failed to show appreciation, but I do mean to say that they are fully as appre-
ciative and much more expressive of their appreciation than
the average white person, particularly where the thing done
is something the motive for which they are able to understand. I have spoken in a great number of their churches,
and in many of their schools, with always one result—a
genuine appreciatior from them of what I was trying to
do. Many of our strongest and best ministers who have
thus attempted to serve, testify to the same responses. In
fact, it is almost pathetic to see the deep appreciation for a
Southern white man who attempts to help them. I recently
spoke in one of the negro churches on St. Helena Island,
South Carolina, and an old woman came up to me and said:
"T'ank de Lord, Southern white man, for sich a one as
you. I nebber thought he would be bawn!" When I assured
her that there were hundreds of other Southern men deeply
interested in the welfare of the race, her gratitude was
unbounded.

> [1]Whut dat you whisperin' keepin' fom me?
> Don't shut me out 'cause I'se ol' an' can't see.
> Somep'n' 's gone wrong dat's a-causin' you dread—
> Don't be afeared to tell—whut! mastah dead?

---

[1]Paul Laurence Dunbar: "Lyrics of the Hearthside," pp. 147-8,

Somebody brung de news early today—
One of de sojers he led, do you say?
Didn't he foller whah ol' mastah led?
How kin he live w'en his leadah is dead?

Let me lay down awhile, dah by his bed;
I wants to t'ink—hit ain't cleah in my head—
Killed while a-leadin' his men into fight—
Dat's whut you said, ain't it, did I hyeah right?

Mastah, my mastah, dead dah in de fiel'?
Lif' me up some—dah, jes' so I kin kneel.
I was too weak to go wid him, dey said,
Well, now I'll—fin' him—so—mastah is dead.

Yes, suh, I's comin' ez fas' ez I kin—
'Twas kin' o' da'k, but hit's lightah agin:
P'omised yo' pappy I'd allus tek keer
Of you—yes, mastah—I's follerin'—hyeah!

Generosity.

The Negro is generous to a fault. Their contributions to their churches are regular and disproportionately large. In any ordinary morning collection they will secure ten times as much in accordance with their wealth as the average white church To their schools they give liberally out of their poverty. I was recently in a town of 3,000 inhabitants where there was being built by taxation a $65,000 public school for the whites. The town owned no school building for the Negroes, though one-third of the population belonged to that race. Enterprising negro men had built a school out of their own means. The white school ran nine months, but there was only sufficient money appropriated to employ negro teachers three months, and again the people subscribed annually enough to extend the term to seven months.

Again and again as I have been on investigation tours I have found homes where they have reared and cared for more orphans than they have had children of their own. In the home of a Baptist minister recently I drew out the information that he had two children of his own, but had reared six orphan children who were not related to him by blood in any way. No Negro will let another suffer so long as he has a crust to share. Whatever others, who are cynical, may call it, I call this generosity.

Without Malice.

Some time ago I had a letter from a prominent plantation owner and manager in the state of Texas. He was expressing the hope that I would put into written form a statement about the real qualities of the Negro. He reminded me that he had never in his long experience with Negroes known one to harbor a revengeful spirit. They may be passionately angry, but their anger soon cools. They forgive and then forget—a thing hard for the white man to do. This is characteristic of the African native just as it is of the American Negro. Dowd says of them: "A few hours or a few days are sufficient to obliterate any resentful impulse they may have had."[1] The long-suffering of the Negro under abuse, and without resentment, marks him out as the most patient race in the world. Abstractly we all admire patience, but as a practical trait of character the Anglo-Saxon is simply incapable of appreciating this fine trait of the Negro.

Kindliness.

In this connection one must not fail to mention the spirit of kindliness which is well nigh a universal characteristic. It is the rarest thing in the world to find a Negro without the milk of human kindness in him. He may have even a vein of cruelty, but side by side with it will be found the most genuine kindliness of spirit. Dr. Booker T. Washington says that patience, kindliness and lack of resentment are the three distinguishing marks of a real Negro.

---

[1] "The Negro Races," p. 396.

Sense of Humor.

One of the saving virtues in difficult and trying situations is a real sense of humor. Because the Indian had not this trait of character he has practically passed away in the hard conflict with the white man. Had the Negro been lacking here he doubtless would never have prospered as he has. "The quaint humor of the Negro helped to turn many a sharp corner. It helped to excuse his mistakes and, by turning a reproof into a jest, to soften the resentment of his master for his faults."[1]

The quick repartee of the Negro is proverbial. I remember once, when I was a student at the university, to have passed two negro waiters with a pair of riding leggins in my hand. One of the Negroes remarked, "Misser Wea'erford gwine gimme them when he leaves college." Quick as a flash the other responded, "Huh, talk lack I done quit wu'kin heah!" There is no better amusement than to sit down near a railroad station where a dozen negroes are congregated and, unobserved, listen to their sallies. It is all so quaint, so naive, and withal so full of genuine humor that it furnishes real recreation.

Religious and Musical.

It is almost unnecessary to call attention to the fact that the Negro is essentially religious. In my former book[2] I have given an entire chapter to this point. On a recent visit to St. Helena Island, South Carolina, I found there were not only seven churches with large memberships, but scattered over the island nearly one hundred praise houses, in which services are held every Tuesday, Thursday, Saturday and Sunday night. Religion is a real part of life with the race and gives promise of a better day to come.

---

[1] "The Story of the Negro," p. 158.
[2] "Negro Life in the South, Chapter V," Association Press, New York.

Likewise, music is the Negro's very breath of life. The most distinctive music that America has produced is negro music. By this he has quieted the negro child, by it he has lightened the burdens of the long day's tasks, and through it he has poured out the deep longings of his soul for freedom. Those who have heard the students at Hampton, Fisk or Tuskegee sing the old plantation melodies have some vague idea of the wild charm of their music and the powerful part it must have played in their lives. Perhaps the Negro does not sing so much now as formerly, but one of the elements of his nature, softening and mellowing all the harsher traits, is that passionate love for music which characterizes every member of the race.

Summary.

What a catalogue of splendid qualities is this: Fidelity amid trying circumstances; gratitude where blessings have been bestowed; forgiving in spirit even when grossly wronged; patient in the face of sore trial; generous in spite of bitter poverty; always seeing the humor of a situation, thus saving many a tragic scene; deeply and intensely religious, even though their religion is often perverted; with souls responsive to the truest of musical rhythm; and, one might truly add, cheerful in the midst of privations; sympathetic to the point of suffering; intensely curious and eager to know. What if the race is not the most brilliantly intellectual? What if they are lacking in self-mastery? What if there is often a lack of industry and thrift?—here is a catalogue of race traits enough to make any race happy, virtuous, useful, and even great.

Not a characteristic has been given which is not commonly found in the masses of the Negroes. Whatever of failures there are, and they are many, whatever of shortcomings and tragedies of life—here is enough to give heart to every genuine friend of the race.

I call upon the negro students who may see this page to unite their efforts to eradicate the weaknesses and foster the virtues of their race. I call upon the white college men who study this to lend a helping hand to a weaker brother. I call on all who believe in the essential value of humanity, who believe in God as a Father of us all, that we shall give ourselves in unselfish service for making the best prevail in the life of this struggling people.

II

NEGRO LEADERSHIP AND THE GROWTH OF RACE PRIDE

ODE TO ETHIOPIA

O Mother Race! to thee I bring
This pledge of faith unwavering,
   This tribute to thy glory.
I know the pangs which thou didst feel,
When Slavery crushed thee with its heel,
   With thy dear blood all gory.

Be proud, my Race, in mind and soul,
Thy name is writ on Glory's scroll
   In characters of fire.
High 'mid the clouds of Fame's bright sky
Thy banner's blazoned folds now fly,
   And truth shall lift them higher.

Thou hast the right to noble pride,
Whose spotless robes were purified
   By blood's severe baptism.
Upon thy brow the cross was laid,
And labor's painful sweat-beads made
   A consecrating chrism.

No other race, or white or black,
When bound as thou wert, to the rack,
   So seldom stooped to grieving;
No other race, when free again,
Forgot the past and proved them men
   So noble in forgiving.

Go on and up! Our souls and eyes
Shall follow thy continued rise;
   Our ears shall list thy story
From bards who from thy root shall spring,
And proudly tune their lyres to sing
   Of Ethiopia's glory.

                              —P. L. Dunbar.

CHAPTER II

NEGRO LEADERSHIP AND THE GROWTH OF RACE PRIDE

INDIVIDUALISM in the sense of isolated endeavor is becoming less and less prevalent in America. The early plantation system, where each was an independent unit in itself and able to supply all its simple needs, has completely lost its place in the industrial economy of our country. This was a type of individualism which finds its opposite at the present time in cooperative creameries, cooperative disposal of crops, cooperative stock breeding, etc. Likewise, individualism in manufacture and commerce is giving way to cooperation. We now have the larger organizations minimizing expense, reaching out over larger territories, bringing together large groups of people in the manufacture, distribution and consumption of the article. If a man desires to do large things today he secures the cooperation of the largest possible number of men in his project. We no longer spend our energy in isolated endeavor, but the best type of individualist is now the man who leads many other individuals in concerted action.

Basis of Cooperation.

The basis of cooperation is like-mindedness, or kindredness of ideas and ideals. Two men do not and cannot work harmoniously together unless they are sufficiently like-minded to be moving in the same direction and toward the same goal. The thief and the honest man soon dissolve partnership. Not only so, but two honest men may find partnership incompatible. Deep down in their natures there may be that fundamental difference of feeling and conception which makes it impossible for the right kind of mutual confidence to spring up. Under such circumstances a business partnership is exceedingly trying.

Likewise in the broader relationships of life there must be that compatibility which arises from mutual confidence. Like-mindedness, kindredness of conception, and genuine confidence are therefore the essentials of cooperation. No group of men who do not believe in themselves and in one another can be expected to cooperate in bringing about large results. It ought to be said that some large outstanding motive often will help to weld into like-mindedness those who otherwise might be incompatible. I recall that during the Spanish-American War a great many public orators referred to the fact that the North and the South had been drawn much closer together in the face of a common peril and a common opportunity.

Race Pride and Racial Cooperation.

This at once leads one to consider what it is that will give to a whole race that cooperative action which will enable it to achieve worthily. The first essential is that the members of the race shall be like-minded, shall come to realize their consciousness of like desires and needs—in other words, shall come into a realization of Kind. This means the growth of race consciousness. It means that men shall come to see that they belong to a common race, have a common heritage and a common future. Nothing can take the place of this. This race consciousness growing into race pride becomes the most powerful factor in welding together, into cooperative and constructive action, all those who belong to the race. It at once raises efficiency and increases determination, and these in turn tend to create a greater self-respect and self-confidence.

Not Segregation.

Race pride, race consciousness, and race cooperation do not mean race segregation. The fact that one is an Anglo-Saxon does not cut him off from interest in and sympathy with the whole world. It simply gives a vantage ground from which the characteristics of other races may be serenely reviewed. A man is more of a world citizen because he is a good American, and likewise a man is more thoroughly sympathetic with humanity because he belongs to, works for, and is a genuine part of, one group of the human family.

Therefore, when we talk about the growth of race pride and race consciousness on the part of the American Negro, we do not mean that he will be less an American, but more a Negro. He is more a Negro that he may be more an American. He is not less interested in humanity because he finds himself interested in his own race, but the very fact of his race appreciation gives him a new consciousness of the dignity of all human kind. Thus it seems clear that if the Negro is ever to become efficient, it must be because he shall come to realize the value and worth of his own race. We cannot hope to make a people worthy so long as they expect to be nothing and do not believe in themselves.

Incentive of Race Success.

Dr. Booker T. Washington in one of his books speaks of how he began reading biography while a student at Hampton, and how he kept wondering why there might not be some negro men who would do great things. His fellow students laughed at him and told him that those of whom he read were white men and that Negroes never could accomplish such results. They were without any race consciousness in the best sense. Certainly, they were without race pride. Perhaps one of the best things Dr. Washington has done for his race is to inspire a real pride and a real belief among his people.

So long as all the virtue is supposed to reside in another race there can be no hope for the Negro. But when he begins to get sufficient culture and sufficient resources to find a larger life within his own race there can be no doubt that he has a motive for progress.

"But build him up, make him sufficient in himself, give him within his own race life that which will satisfy, and the social question will be solved. The trained Negro is less and less inclined to lose himself and his race in the sea of another race. As he develops, he is finding a new race-consciousness, he is building a new race pride. He no longer objects to being called a Negro—it is becoming the badge of his race and the mark of his self-sufficiency. We have nothing, therefore, to fear from giving him a chance."[1]

Indications of Growth in Race Consciousness.

It is therefore with the keenest interest that one looks everywhere for indications that this pride of race is growing, and one hails with delight anything that points to its fuller development. Perhaps one of the clearest indications of this new appreciation of the race is the open avowal and championship of the race in its needs by the better type of Negroes. To me it is significant that a man of the capacity and influence of Dr. Booker T. Washington should go out of his way to assert over and over again his glory in his own race.

"What I have said here of my own feelings in regard to my race is representative of the feelings of thousands of others of the black people of this country. Adverse criticism has driven them to think deeper than they otherwise would about the problems which confront them as a race, to cling closer than they otherwise would have done to their own people, to value more highly than they once did, the songs and records of their past life in slavery. The effect

---

[1] The Author's "Negro Life in the South," pp. 173-174.

has been to give them, in short, that sort of race pride and race consciousness which, it seems to me, they need to bring out and develop the best that is in them. . . . Perhaps it will not be out of place for me to say here, at the beginning of this book, that the more I have studied the masses of the race to which I belong, the more I have learned not only to sympathize with but to respect them. I am proud and happy to be identified with their struggle for a higher and better life."[1]

Paul Laurence Dunbar has done the race a real service through his poems and stories, which are so genuine, so true to life, and yet so filled with a deep appreciation of the value of his own people, that one cannot read his works without coming to have a new conception of the Negro. Here and there you can find a Negro, who is more white than black, and who chafes under conditions, but it is remarkable how large a proportion of the negro writers and public men of our day glory in their own race.

New Appreciation of Their Past.

Another indication of the growth of race pride and race consciousness is the manner in which the best Negroes glory in their past. There was a time when the Negro was ashamed of his slavery; there was a time when he was unwilling to talk of his relationship to Africa, and thought the farther he could get away from his past the better off he would be. In fact, I have had a letter within a year from a leading Northern gentleman telling me of a negro quartette. In this letter the chief recommendation of the quartette was that it did not sing the old melodies because the singers wanted to forget the past. To me that is the worst condemnation that could have Leen written. The boy who goes away from his simple, ignorant, but honest home, enters the university, and with his new culture learns

---

[1]"The Story of the Negro," pp. 12 and 15.

to despise the old home and the parents, proves himself
thereby a man of small caliber. The race that is ashamed
to own its past, that wants to forget the conditions from
which it sprang, is a weak race. There are some negroes
of this type—those whom Dr. Washington calls the "intel-
lectuals"—but the mass of the race is coming to appreciate
the strength, the fidelity, the glory of its fathers, and they
are clinging more tenaciously to their traditions. One of
the splendid things about Hampton and Tuskegee is the
fact that every student is taught to glory in the history of
his people. Not to be proud of its failures, of course, but to
be proud of the fact that in those earlier generations there
was that latent capacity which, bequeathed to the present
generation, makes progress possible.

Negro Music.

The most distinctive music of America is the old plantation melodies. Wherever Negroes sing these in the real
spirit, without being ashamed of them—as I have found
to be the case in one or two schools—there is a richness
of harmony and a depth of soul that is possessed by no
other music that I have heard. Even the children at the
Penn School on St. Helena Island, led by the clear, rich
voice of one of their own number, put such splendid feeling into one of these old spirituals as to transport one out
of himself into a world where manhood and womanhood
win the final victory in the long struggle with suffering.
It seems to me almost criminal that the negro children in
the public schools are not taught more of these old melodies.
They voice the feeling of a past age, to be sure, but an age
which should not be allowed to pass from memory. Here
it should be mentioned that some of the best negro musi-
cians are building on the basis of these old spirituals to
make a music suited to the Negro of this day. One of the
best illustrations of this that I have heard is a splendid

piece of music based on the old song, "Swing Low, Sweet Chariot," written by Professor Smith, the bandmaster at Tuskegee, and rendered by the student band. This, in my judgment, is one of the finest ways of cultivating this race pride and race consciousness which is just bursting into bloom.

Collection of Books and Pictures.

Another indication of the growth of race pride is the fact that Negroes in an increasing number are now diligently collecting all the old manuscripts, books, pictures etc., that bear on the history of the race. They are getting anxious to know more of their past, to understand the motives that actuated their forefathers, to live over in sympathetic feeling the old days, the events of which have stamped themselves indelibly on the race. Mr. Moorland, of Washington, one of the secretaries of the Colored Men's Department of the Young Men's Christian Association, has been one of the most industrious and successful collectors of such material, concerning the Negro's past history. It is altogether likely that he has the best private library of this kind now in existence. A number of the negro colleges have secured very valuable collections through similar sources. Not only are these people interested in the history of the past, but many of them are diligent collectors of materials showing the present successes and progress of their group. Thus you will find Dr. Booker T. Washington's books in many of the humble homes, because not only of his career, but because of what he says of negro progress, in which he holds out a real hope to all who are struggling upward.

Growth of Business Interest.

Another indication of the growth of race pride is the large variety of business enterprises which are springing up all over the South, the largest asset of which is this desire of the common people to favor their own race. There are literally scores of insurance companies, fifty-six banks, drug stores unnumbered, barber shops, livery stables, mercantile establishments, printing houses, newspapers and periodicals circulated among Negroes alone, a negro doll factory and a negro calendar factory.

Many of these business enterprises, such as barber shops, drug stores and mercantile establishments are patronized by the whites as well as the blacks. But the fact that the Negroes have their own business houses and that they have confidence in them is a clear indication of a new race consciousness. In similar manner, the increasing number of negro physicians, dentists and lawyers, who get a good practice among their own people, proves that the race is beginning to believe in itself. It has not been many years since a Negro would have laughed at the idea that another Negro could do the medical work in his home. They had no confidence in the ability of one of their own race to meet their professional needs. But this is changing rapidly, and the time is not far distant when the mass of the Negroes will look to their own race for the most of their medical, dental and legal advice.

Negro Dolls and Negro Calendars.

One of the most interesting signs of race pride is to be found in the large number of real negro dolls to be seen in the best homes. These dolls are more expensive than the white dolls, because they are not made in such large quantities, and it is only within the last few years that there has been a demand for the same. Dr. R. H. Boyd, of the National Baptist Publishing House,[1] has recently established a large trade in these dolls. In order to get manufactured negro dolls true to life, and not simply caricatures,

[1] See the Author's "Negro Life in the South," pp. 52-54.

he made a personal visit to the German factories, furnished them with hundreds of pictures of real Negroes and insisted on having real likenesses. The result has been a very prosperous business in these dolls. When I was in Dr. Boyd's office soon after Christmas a year ago I saw a great number of checks being returned to merchants all over the South who had ordered these dolls in much larger numbers than could be supplied. Recently I have talked with the manager of this department, and he told me the house had sold two carloads of these dolls during the Christmas holidays of 1911. Twenty-five years ago negro parents were unwilling for their children to have negro dolls, but now they are willing to pay an extra price for them. This is a clear indication of a growing race consciousness. In like manner, a negro calendar factory in Louisville, Ky., is doing a thriving business.

Pride in Race Leadership.

Perhaps the most encouraging feature of the whole situation is the pride which Negroes have in the leadership of their own blood. A Southern white woman teaching a Sunday School class of negro boys started to tell a story recently of a boy who had succeeded. One of the negro boys stopped her by saying: "Please, miss, is it a white boy you're talking about? If it is, we don't want to hear it."

Are There Leaders Without Caucasian Ancestry?

In the beginning of this paragraph I wish to make it clear, that I do not for one moment discount those splendid leaders of the race who have a mixed ancestry. They are a noble band and are doing a noble work, making a contribution not only to their own race, but perhaps to all races. One of the common sayings is, however, that the men who are leaders of the negro race are all of mixed blood and get their powers of initiative and leadership from the white race. Perhaps this feeling has been somewhat accentuated by the fact that Douglas and Washington and a number of the more prominent leaders have been men of mixed ancestry. But many of these men came into places of leadership, partly because of their more favored training, and not alone because of their ability. It ought further to be said that some of the best of these leaders, such as Dr. Washington, while they have white blood in their veins, are real Negroes in inheritance, in temper and feeling. No one who knows Dr. Washington could for one moment doubt that his mother—a slave woman—stamped her life indelibly upon him. But there are many leaders of the race, perhaps not so prominent as Washington, but of the same fiber of efficiency and ability, who can trace their ancestry and show no strain of white blood.

Major R. R. Moton.

The first man in this class to whom any man's mind would readily turn in naming such a list is Major R. R. Moton, the commandant and disciplinarian at Hampton Institute. It has been my good fortune to come to know Major Moton quite well in the visits I have made to Hampton. He is one of the few men in America who can trace their ancestry on both sides in unbroken line across the seas. His great-grandfather was an African chief, and the Major's splendid bearing indicates that he has lost none of his ancestor's regal qualities. I have heard more than one Southern white man say that Major Moton was the sanest and strongest representative of the negro race they had ever met. Others have said to me that he is the best speaker— white or black—they have ever heard, and yet he does not claim to be a speaker at all. He has a clear head, a noble heart, and a manly bearing which at once convince you that he has a message worth while and is not afraid to give it.

Major Moton holds a most delicate position at Hampton. In the college community there are pure Negroes, mulattoes, Indians, Northern white people, Southern white people—all working for the same great cause—the elevation of the race. It is no easy matter to harmonize all of these types, and yet so rare is his tact and so true is his judgment that each group gives him enthusiastic support. Washington has said of him: "It has been through contact with men like Major Moton that I have received a kind of education no books could impart."[1] It would be worth a trip to Hampton just to know Major Moton. If more of our Southern white people could see him, so calm, so unostentatious, so unpresuming, and yet so efficient and thorough, they would never say again that the negro race could not produce a pure-blood leader.

George W. Carver.

Another negro educator, whom I have known for eighteen years, is Professor Carver, of Tuskegee. He is simple, modest, retiring, and yet clearly confident when talking in terms of his specialty. He knows his business and soon convinces you that he knows it. Of him Sir Henry Johnston, in his very full volume, "The Negro in the New World," says: "Professor Carver, who teaches scientific agriculture, botany, agricultural chemistry, etc., is, as regards complexion and features, an absolute Negro; but in cut of clothes, the accent of his speech, the soundness of his science, he might be professor of science, not at Tuskegee, but at Oxford or Cambridge."[2]

Dr. Joseph C. Price.

Or to take one more example of a leader in negro education, one would readily turn to Dr. Joseph Price, the first President of Livingston College, in North Carolina. He

---

[1]"My Larger Education," p. 219.
[2]"The Negro in the New World," p. 416.

was born a slave in North Carolina five years before the opening of the Civil War; was educated at Lincoln University; was ordained as an elder in the A. M. E. Church; served in the General Conference of that body for 1880; was appointed by the President of the United States to a post of foreign honor, which he refused; was a representative for his church in England at the Ecumenical Conference of 1881, where he laid the foundation for the establishment of Livingston College, to which he gave the remainder of his life. His successor has said of him:[1] "He was no self-seeker. He did not labor for the notice of society or the prizes of the world, but the one controlling idea of his life was to lift his race out of ignorance and moral degradation into which the misfortune of a cruel past had sunk them, and to lead them to higher planes of intelligence and social refinement. He was forcible in his appeals for justice and fair dealing, honest in his statements and true to his convictions, yet he carried no gall in his nature. No bitterness escaped his lips. There was no rancor in his bosom. He had faith in the power of Christ to eradicate the evils of society. He believed in the ultimate triumph of truth and righteousness and was satisfied that the evils of society will be rooted out." Dr. Booker T. Washington called him "by all odds the leading and most prominent man of his race in North Carolina and one of the most eloquent men in the country."[2]

Leaders in Business Life.

There are two very interesting men in business life in the South about whom I ought to say a word. One is Isaiah Montgomery and the other is Charles Banks. Isaiah Montgomery was the slave of Joseph Davis, the brother of President Jefferson Davis of the Confederacy. Both of

[1]Grogman's "Progress of a Race," pp. 523-524.
[2]"The Story of the Negro," p. 24.

the Davis brothers were the best type of slave owners. They were kindly in the fullest degree to their slaves, gave them a practical form of self-government, allowed them much of free time to work for themselves, gave the brighter ones a chance to acquire some education, and in every way looked after their permanent welfare. The father of Isaiah Montgomery learned to read and write on the plantation of Joseph Davis, and after the war the father and two sons bought the old plantation at a price of three hundred thousand dollars. In 1890 Isaiah Montgomery was the man who led a party of negro men up the Mississippi Delta to the place now known as Mound Bayou, and there they cleared the forest and started the present negro town. Mound Bayou has a bank, a number of cotton gins, a telephone exchange, a newspaper, and, I believe, waterworks and electric lights. There are between four and five thousand inhabitants, all Negroes, and they own about 30,000 acres of land. To have founded such a town; to have brought it to its present state of efficiency; to be able to have the type of law and order the citizens have—these things mark out this man as one of genuine leadership. Associated with Montgomery in this work has been a much younger though no less forceful man, Charles Banks, banker, cotton broker, real estate dealer, head of a large corporation for erecting a big cotton oil mill, and planter. Dr. Booker T. Washington has described him so much better than anyone else could, I quote two paragraphs from his statement:[1]

"I have been watching him do things, watching him grow, and as I have studied him more closely my admiration for this big, quiet, graceful giant has steadily increased. One thing that has always impressed itself upon me in regard to Mr. Banks is the fact that he never claims credit for doing anything that he can give credit to other people

---

[1] "My Larger Education," pp. 207-208.

for doing. He has never made an effort to make himself prominent. He simply prefers to get a job done, and if he can use other people and give them credit for doing the work, he is happy to do so.

"At the present time Charles Banks is not, by any means, the wealthiest, but I think I am safe in saying that he is the most influential negro business man in the United States. He is the leading negro banker in Mississippi, where there are eleven negro banks, and he is Secretary and Treasurer of the large benefit association in that State—namely, that attached to the Masonic order—which paid death claims in 1910 to the amount of one hundred and ninety-five thousand dollars and had a cash balance of eighty thousand dollars. He organized and has been the moving spirit in the State organization of the Business League in Mississippi, and has been for a number of years the Vice-President of the National Negro Business League."

"Charles Banks is, however, more than a successful business man. He is a leader of his race and a broad-minded and public-spirited citizen. Although he holds no public office, and, so far as I know, has no desire to do so, there are, in my opinion, few men, either white or black, in Mississippi today who are performing, directly or indirectly, a more important service to their State than Charles Banks."

Literary Leadership.

If one had space it would be well to say a word about Phillis Wheatley, that native African girl brought to Boston as a slave child, with scarcely more than a loin cloth for clothes, and bought by a kindly Boston woman at the slave market. Her verses are such as to prove the latent literary possibilities of the race. Well can we pass to consider Paul Laurence Dunbar as the best type of nego poet. The parents of Dunbar were pure-blood Negroes, slaves in Kentucky. Before the war, the father ran away to Canada and the mother followed on to Dayton, Ohio, where the son was born. He grew up in the midst of the most dire poverty, the father dying while the son was the merest child. When old enough to work, he became an elevator boy, at which work he did some of his earliest composing. William Dean Howells says of his work:

"What struck me in reading Mr. Dunbar's poetry was what had already struck his friends in Ohio and Indiana, in Kentucky and Illinois. They had felt, as I felt, that, however gifted his race had proven itself in music, in oratory, in several of the other arts, here was the first instance of an American Negro who had evinced innate distinction in literature. In my criticism of his book I had alleged Dumas in France, and I had forgetfully failed to allege the far greater Pushkin in Russia; but these were both mulattoes, who might have been supposed to derive their qualities from white blood vastly more artistic than ours, and who were the creatures of an environment more favorable to their literary development. So far as I could remember, Paul Dunbar was the only man of pure African blood and of American civilization to feel the negro life aesthetically and express it lyrically. It seemed to me that this had come to its most modern consciousness in him, and that his brilliant and unique achievement was to have studied the American Negro objectively, and to have represented him as he found him to be, with humor, with sympathy, and yet with what the reader must instinctively feel to be the entire truthfulness. I said that a race which had come to this effect in any member of it, had attained civilization in him, and I permitted myself the imaginative prophecy that the hostilities and the prejudices which had so long constrained his race were destined to vanish in the arts; that these were to be the final proof that God had made of one blood all nations of men. I thought his merits positive, and not comparative; and I held that if his black poems had been written by a white man, I should not have found them less admirable. I accepted them as an evidence of the essential unity of the human race, which does not think or feel black in one and white in another, but humanly in all. . . . He has at least produced something that, however we may critically disagree about it, we cannot well refuse to enjoy; in more than one piece he has produced a work of art." [1]

I have read with great care all of Dunbar's four volumes of poems and his several volumes of stories. Many of them are very charming. What is most interesting to me about them is the keen appreciation they show of the traits of negro character. They are intensely human, so full of the every-day experiences, that they possess a charm all their own. What could be more human and real than this: [2]

> "Den you men's de mule's ol' ha'ness,
>   An' you men's de broken chair.
> Hummin' all de time you's wo'kin'
>   Some ol' common kind o' air.
> Evah now an' then you looks out,
>   Tryin' mighty ha'd to frown,
> But you cain't, you's glad hit's rainin',
>   An' dey's time to tinker 'roun'."

Or what is there that betrays the changing moods of the Negro more clearly or more beautifully than this: [3]

> "An' my wife an' all de othahs—
>   Male an' female, small an' big—
> Even up to gray-haired granny,
>   Seems jes' boun' to do a jig;
> 'Twell I change the style o' music,
>   Change de movement an' de time,
> An' de ringin' little banjo
>   Plays an ol' hea't-feelin' hime."

Although Dunbar never lived in the South, he received from his mother not only a knowledge of Southern conditions, but such a sympathetic feeling for its life that he has done more than any other Negro to give a right setting to

[1] Introduction to "Lyrics of Lowly Life," XVI, XVII, XX.
[2] "Lyrics of the Hearthside," p. 141.
[3] "Lyrics of Lowly Life," p. 43.

its joys and tragedies. Here is a sample of this genuine understanding of the old conditions and the old Negro:[1]

"Dey have lef' de ole plantation to de swallers,
  But it hol's in me a lover till de las';
Fu' I fin' hyeah in de memory dat follers
  All dat loved me an' dat I loved in de pas'.

So I'll stay an' watch de deah ole place an' tend it
  Ez I used to in de happy days gone by.
'Twell de otah Mastah thinks it's time to end it,
  An' calls me to my qua'ters in de sky."

He has also a deep sympathy which enters into the mood of the Negro as perhaps no white man ever could. What could be more tender and beautiful than this:[2]

"Two little boots all rough an' wo',
  Two little boots.
Laws, I's kissed 'em times befo',
  Dese little boots.
Seems de toes a-peepin' thoo'
Dis hyeah hole an' sayin' 'Boo,'
Evah time dey looks at you—
  Dese little boots.

"Membah de time he put 'em on,
  Dese little boots;
Riz an' called fu' 'em by dawn,
  Dese little boots;
Den he tromped the livelong day,
Laffin' in his happy way,
Evaht'ing he had to say,
  'My little boots.'

"Kickin' the san' de whole day long,
  Dem little boots;
Good de cobblah made 'em strong,
  Dem little boots!
Rocks was fu' dat baby's use,
I'on had to stan' abuse
W'en you tu'ned dese champeens loose,
  Dese little boots!

"Use to make de ol' cat cry,
  Dese little boots;
Den you walked it mighty high,
  Proud little boots!

[1] "Lyrics of Lowly Life," p. 160.
[2] "Lyrics of Love and Laughter," pp. 1-3.

Abms akimboo, stan'in' wide,
Eyes a-sayin' 'Dis is pride!'
Den de manny-baby stride!
    You little boots.

"Somehow you don' seem so gay,
    Po' little boots,
Sence yo' ownah went away.
    Po' little boots!
Yo' bright tops don' look so red,
Dese brass tips is dull an' dead;
"Goo-by," what de baby said;
    Deah little boots!

"Ain't you kin' o' sad yo'se'f,
    You little boots?
Dis is all his mam's lef',
    Two little boots.
Sence huh baby gone an' died,
Heaven itse'f hit seem to hide
Des a little bit inside
    Two little boots."

Or what goes right to the heart of the old Southern love on the part of the child for the Negro, and that of the Negro for the child, like this: [1]

"Little mas' a-axin'
    'Who is Santy Claus?'
Meks it kin' o' taxin'
    Not to brek de laws.
Chillun's pow'ful tryin'
    To a pusson's grace
W'en dey go a pryin'
    Right on th'oo you' face
Down among yo' feelin's;
    Jes' 'pears lak dat you
Got to change you' dealin's
    So's to tell 'em true."[1]

One of the charming elements in all of Dunbar's work is its freedom from any cynicism or bitterness. Born of slave parents, rocked in the cradle of dire poverty, struggling into manhood through the grind of a daily task which made it next to impossible for him to get that knowledge for which his soul thirsted—such a person one would not

---

[1] "Lyrics of the Hearthside," p. 201.

have been surprised to hear carping about the hardships and disappointments of life. Instead of that, there is the most heroic note running all through his writings, and one never puts them down but that he feels himself a little better for having read them. Any race might well be proud of having produced a Dunbar.

Ministerial Leadership.

Dr. Charles T. Walker was born a slave in Richmond County, Georgia, in 1859. His father was his master's coachman, a very religious man, deacon in the little slave Baptist Church organized at Hepsibah, 1848. Several of his uncles were preachers. Left an orphan at eight, becoming a Christian at fourteen, working his way painfully through the public schools, he finally entered the Theological Institute at Augusta, Georgia. Licensed to preach at eighteen, he became the pastor of his home church at Hepsibah. He was for a number of years the pastor of Mount Olivet Baptist Church in New York City, and is now pastor of the Tabernacle Baptist Church, Augusta, Georgia. Not only is he a preacher of great power, but he has fostered education and journalism among his people. He was one of the founders of the Baptist Institute of Augusta, is a trustee of Atlanta Baptist College, helped in the founding of the Augusta Sentinel, has written books on travel, etc. It was due to the effort of Dr. Walker and a few other Negroes that the Georgia State Colored Fair was established. While a pastor in New York he helped in the establishment of a Colored Young Men's Christian Association with five hundred members. He was the man chosen by the International Convention of the Young Men's Christian Association to represent his race in an address at that gathering in Toronto, Canada, 1910. His address was simple, sane, masterful. It had a power of conviction and a deep passion of earnestness which gripped the heart and conscience of those hundreds of white men assembled from every corner of America. He has a sparkling wit, a fine sense of humor, a remarkable ability in story-telling, but with it all that genuine sense of the bigness of life which makes him a power when speaking either to white or colored men. President Taft has said of him that he is the most eloquent man to whom he has ever listened. I could not better prove his sanity and his right to leadership than to quote what Washington says in his motto: "I have determined never to be guilty of ingratitude, never to desert a friend, and never to strike back at an enemy." I have heard Dr. Walker speak both to Northern and Southern men, and, so far as I have ever been able to learn, he lives up to his motto.

George W. Clinton.

I can give space to only one more leader. Bishop Clinton, of the A. M. E. Zion Church, was born a slave in South Carolina, was graduated from the University of South Carolina with the class of 1874, at the time when Negro students were admitted to that institution. Washington says of him:[1]

"Bishop Clinton has done a great service to the denomination to which he belongs, and his years of service have brought him many honors and distinctions. He founded the African Methodist Episcopal Zion Quarterly Review, and edited for a time another publication of the African Methodist Episcopal Conferences at home and abroad. He is a trustee of Livingstone College, Chairman of the Publishing Board, has served as a member of the International Convention of Arbitration, and is Vice-President of the International Sunday School Union.

"Bishop Clinton is a man of a very different type from the other men of pure African blood I have mentioned.

[1]"My Larger Education," pp. 220, 222, 223.

'Although he says he is fifty years of age, he is, in appearance and manner, the youngest man in the group. An erect, commanding figure, with a high, broad forehead, rather refined features, and fresh, frank, almost boyish manner, he is the kind of man who everywhere wins confidence and respect.

"Although Bishop Clinton is by profession a minister and has been all his life in the service of the church, he is, of all the men I have named, the most aggressive in his manner and the most soldierly in his bearing. . . .

"I first made the acquaintance of Bishop Clinton when he came to Tuskegee in 1893 as representative of the African Methodist Episcopal Zion Church at the dedication of the Phelps Hall Bible Training School. The next year he came to Tuskegee as one of the lecturers in that school, and he has spent some time at Tuskegee every year since then, assisting in the work of that institution.

"Bishop Clinton has been of great assistance to us, not only in our work at Tuskegee, but in the larger work we have been trying to do in arousing interest throughout the country in the Negro. He organized in Carolina in 1910 what I think was the most successful educational campaign I have yet been able to make in any of the Southern States."

Summary.

In this brief sketch of negro leadership of pure blood, I have passed over many who are equally prominent and scores of others equally efficient, though less prominent. I have not spoken of R. R. Wright, of Georgia, perhaps the most influential Negro in the State, student, prolific writer on economic questions, President of the State Industrial Normal, a real power in the negro State Fair. He is the one who, as a boy, when asked what message should be given to the white people about the Negroes, said: "Tell them we are rising." Nor have I found space to mention as conspicuous a leader as Alexander Crummell, the great missionary to Liberia; or Lott Cary; or Lucy Laney, the industrial educator of women in Georgia; or M. C. B. Mason, the Secretary of the Freedman's Aid Society; or Bishop Tyree, of Nashville; or Virginia Randolph, who, though obscure as to reputation, has proved herself so much a leader as to have practically transformed all the rural schools of Henrico County, Virginia.

It has not been possible to say anything about T. C. Walker, who graduated from Hampton twenty-five years ago, went back to Gloucester County, Virginia, and began a crusade among his people for sobriety and decency, for buying land, building homes, erecting schools, etc. The outcome is that seven thousand negroes now own one thousand eight hundred and fifty-seven farm plots in that county—an average of a farm plot for every family in the county. Very few live in one-roomed houses; I did not see one in a three days' drive through the country. They have good schools and good churches. They have run whiskey practically out of the country, and during the year 1910 there were only six convictions for serious crimes among the Negroes of the county. These were for shooting, cutting and stealing. All this has come largely through the efforts of Tom Walker, farmer, lawyer, Sunday school worker, reformer and citizen. How many hundreds of white counties in the South need a white man who can and will do for the white farmers what Walker has done for the negro farmers of Gloucester County?

If space would permit, one might wisely speak of D. W. Davis, the author of the poems entitled "Weh Down Souf;" of William Washington Brown; of Edward Wilbur Blyden, the scholar; of Wood, the inventor; of J. H. Smith, United States Minister to Liberia; of Miss Georgia Washington, Mt. Meigs, Ala., and others.

Enough has been said and sufficient examples given to

prove that the negro race can and does produce leaders of unmixed blood. As fast as the race has a chance it will produce more. These examples have been taken from sufficiently varied fields to show that they are not freaks of nature any more than are the leaders of another race. It proves to me that the negro race has capacity for leadership, perhaps not of the same degree or of the same quality as the Anglo-Saxon, but capacity suited to its own needs.

What he needs now is encouragement. We need to hold up to him the splendid examples of those who have succeeded. We need to help him to a new confidence in himself. The books he reads should place his own leaders to the front in order that others of the race may aspire to that fellowship. Even if it were true that the negro race has no leaders save its mixed-bloods, it would do no good constantly to throw this into their faces. What good does it do to tell a boy he has always been a failure, is now a failure, and will always be a failure? Will that help him overcome? Not at all. It simply hardens him in his indifference. And yet that is what many a thoughtless white person has been doing with the Negro for all these years. Even if it were true that they have no pure-blood leaders, we ought to have a better knowledge of human nature than to continue reiterating this to them.

But it is distinctly and positively not true. Outside of two men—Booker T. Washington and Frederick Douglas—the Negroes of unmixed blood can show a right to claim equal rank among the sanest and best leaders of the race. And this is true in spite of the fact that the mixed-blood Negro has had—because of accident of birth—three chances to the black man's one chance for developing leadership.

Recognition of Growing Race Consciousness.

What we need today is a full, glad recognition on the part of the white people of this growing race consciousness and race leadership among Negroes. We need to encourage them to take pride in themselves. We need to give them leadership among their own people just as fast as they are able to take it. We need to make them self-sufficient in themselves just as rapidly as possible. To refuse to recognize their merits and to close our eyes to the facts of real leadership—this simply prolongs the day of the Negro's worthlessness and lack of ambition, proves the white man lacking in statesmanship, and publishes to the world our narrowness and littleness of soul.

CHAPTER III

NEGRO POPULATION AND RACE MOVEMENTS

THE SLAVE'S COMPLAINT

Am I sadly cast aside,
On misfortune's rugged tide?
Will the world my pains deride
    Forever?

Must I dwell in Slavery's night,
And all pleasure take its flight.
Far beyond my feeble sight,
    Forever?

Worst of all, must hope grow dim,
And withhold her cheering beam?
Rather let me sleep and dream
    Forever!

Something still my heart surveys,
Groping through the dreary maze;
Is it Hope?—then burn and blaze
    Forever:

Leave me not a wretch confined,
Altogether lame and blind—
Unto gross despair consigned,
    Forever:

Heaven! in whom I confide;
Canst thou not for all provide?
Condescend to be my guide
    Forever!

And when this transient life shall end,
Oh, may some kind, eternal friend
Bid me from servitude ascend,
    Forever!

—By a Slave.

CHAPTER III

NEGRO POPULATION AND RACE MOVEMENTS

Dr. Booker T. Washington, writing in 1899, said: "I think I am pretty safe in predicting that the census to be taken in 1900 will show that there are not far from ten millions of people of African descent in the United States." [1]

Mr. Thomas Nelson Page, writing in 1904, says: "The negro race has already doubled three times in the United States since the beginning of the last century, and, unless conditions change, it is possible that there may be between sixty and eighty millions of Negroes in this country during the century." [2]

During the same year (1904) there appeared a book by Dr. W. B. Smith, of Tulane University, which attempted with seeming satisfaction to prove that the Negro will soon be a negligible quantity. "It is demonstrated," says Dr. Smith, "that in these two focal regions of the African strength not only is that strength relatively decreasing, but it is decreasing faster and faster. The hour cometh when neither by the ocean nor by the gulf will it signify more than it now does in Philadelphia or New York." [3]

Thus we are immediately faced with absolutely diverse opinions about the future growth of the race problem. Mr. Wilcox, of the United States Bureau of Statistics, thinks that twenty-five millions of Negroes is a liberal estimate for the year 2000.

[1] "Future of American Negro," p. 5.
[2] "The Negro the Southerner's Problem," p. 289.
[3] "The Color Line," p. 204.

The impression made on one by the reading of the arguments of the statisticians concerning the far future (Dr. Smith and Mr. Wilcox) is that a good part of their labor is necessarily guesswork and cannot be otherwise. The censuses of 1870 and of 1890 are allowed by all authorities to be very inaccurate, and earlier figures are none too certain. Besides, there are no figures of marriages and births in past census records, and all the death-rate figures are exceedingly questionable. To make predictions on such uncertain foundations is, therefore, hazardous in the extreme.

One thing, however, can be asserted with some degree of certainty, and that is that the relative increase of Negroes has gradually declined during the past century, and these facts are still borne out by the census of 1910. The following table shows the per cent of increase for Negroes according to double census periods since 1800:

1800-1820	76.8 per cent
1720-1840	62.2 per cent
1840-1860	54.6 per cent
1860-1880	48.2 per cent
1880-1900	34.2 per cent
1900-1910	11.3 per cent

The increase from 1890-1900 was 18 per cent, so that the last census shows a decrease in accordance with all the figures of the past century. The remarkable thing about these figures is the fact that there seems to be a hastening process in the relative decrease of the Negro. There are three States in the South where the Negroes actually decreased in numbers between 1900 and 1910. These are Tennessee, Kentucky and Maryland. It will be noted that these are border States, and one would readily suppose that this decrease is due to migration. The census returns are not sufficiently advanced to make it possible for one to locate the places to which these Negroes have migrated. There are small relative decreases in the proportion of Negroes to whites in all the other Southern States save three—Oklahoma, Arkansas and West Virginia. These three States show a larger per cent of increase among Negroes than among whites. In 1900 the Negro constituted 32.3 per cent of the population of the South Atlantic and South Central States. In 1910 he constituted only 29.8 per cent, showing a decided falling off. One factor entering into this relative decrease of the Negro is that of emigration of Negroes to the North and the immigration of Northern whites to the South. The figures for 1910 on these points are not yet available, but it is quite certain that the tendency will be similar to that of the past two or three decades. In 1890 there were 1,038,000 Southern whites living in other States outside of the South, and in 1900 the number had increased to 1,116,000, a gain of 88,000. In 1890 there were 582,000 non-Southern white Americans living in the South, and in 1900 the number was 725,000, a gain of 143,000. Therefore it will be seen that the loss of whites over the number coming in is a decreasing quality. The net loss of whites by this migration in 1890 being 456,000, and in 1900 being 390,000.

On the other hand, the number of Negroes leaving the South is an increasing quantity. In 1890 there were 241,000 Southern-born Negroes (counting all men as whites and Negroes which is sufficiently accurate) living in other than Southern States, and in 1900 there were 349,000. The total Negro population in other than Southern States was in 1900 911,025, and in 1910 it was 1,078,804. The number of Northern Negroes coming South during the decade was only 2,100. It will readily be seen, therefore, that this migration affects the relative increase of Negroes and whites in the South in favor of the latter race.

The increase of negro population in the Southern States during the last decade has been only 10.4 per cent, while for the whole country it has been 11.3 per cent. The increase

for Southern whites has been 24.4 per cent, while the increase for the whole country has been only 22.3 per cent.
It is actually true, therefore, that the South is becoming
whiter.

Movement Cityward.

Another partial explanation of the relative (not actual)
decrease of the Negro in the South is the movement cityward.   In the nine cotton States of the South—Alabama,
Arkansas, Florida, Georgia, Louisiana, Mississippi, North
Carolina, South Carolina and Tennessee (unfortunately,
the figures for Texas are not yet available)—the white
population in cities has been increasing as follows: In 1890
there were 11.6 per cent living in city areas; in 1900, 14
per cent; in 1910, 18.9 per cent. The corresponding figures
for negro population in these States are: 1890, 11.8 per
cent; 1900, 14.7 per cent; 1910, 17.7 per cent. Thus the
city population of the whites has increased in proportion
by 7.2 per cent and that of the Negroes by 5.8 per cent. It
will thus be seen that both the white and the colored races
are moving toward the city, though the cityward movement
for whites is greater than that for Negroes.

Now, the significant fact about this migration as it
relates to the Negro lies in his poorer health conditions in
the city as compared with the white man. So long as he
lives in the country he at least has good ventilation and
usually better sanitation than he has in the city. The Negro
has practically the monoply of the unsanitary and disease-
breeding sections of the city, while most of the whites in
the South live under more favorable conditions. This
shows in the very high death rate of the city Negro. Among
them the infant mortality is almost 50 per cent in
some cities, and tuberculosis and venereal troubles take off
literally thousands. It can readily be seen that the city is

the Negro's enemy, and has much to do with his declining rate of increase in population.

Death Rate of Both Races.

As stated before, there are no whole or complete statistics on the death rate of either whites or blacks. There are, however, certain regions—mainly cities—where the local authorities attempt to keep records of deaths. This so-called registration area included 13.4 per cent of the Negroes in the United States in 1900, and, being almost entirely urban, cannot be considered as entirely true as to the facts of the whole race. There are almost no records for the rural population where the great mass of Negroes live. The following table shows the relative death rate of the two races in these registration areas, 1900:

RACE	1900		
	Population	Number Deaths	Death Rate
Negro	1,180,546	35,710	30.2
White	27,555,800	474,640	17.3

The corresponding figures for 1890 are 29.9 for Negroes and 19.1 for whites. This figure for Negroes includes a few Mongolians and Indians, and perhaps the death rate should not be for Negroes alone more than 29. This means that for every thousand Negroes twenty-nine die annually. Unfortunately, the death rates for 1910 are not yet available, though workers in the Census Bureau estimate the death rate will be less than 28 for Negroes. So far as any conclusion can be drawn from these figures, it is seen that the negro death rate is almost twice as high as that for the white. It must always be remembered that these figures apply only to the city population for certain sections, and hence are apt to be much higher for the Negro than such figures would be for the country districts. We can only surmise that the death rate in the country wou'd likely be larger for Negroes than whites, but how much larger we cannot tell.

Birth Rate.

Inasmuch as there are no reliable figures for births, the best substitute is to find the number of children under five years of age to all females between fifteen and forty-four years of age. This relative number of children to women of the age of motherhood will help to indicate the relative fecundity of the two races. The following table, based on the last three census periods and divided as to sections of the country, is quite illuminative:

| CENSUS YEAR | Number of children under five years of age to 1,000 females fifteen to forty-four years of age. | | | | | |
| | Continental U. S. | | South Atlantic States | | South Central States | |
	Negro Indian andMongolian population	White Population	Negro Indian andMongolian population	White Population	Negro Indian andMongolian population	White Population
1880............	759	586	787	666	799	749
1890............	616	517	638	587	659	655
1900............	585	508	630	595	612	659

The above figures include all non-Caucasians among the colored population, but since this is less than one per cent of the colored population in the South Atlantic and South Central divisions, the error would be insignificant. It will be noted that in the United States as a whole the number of children for both races has declined rapidly, but much more rapidly among the Negroes than among the whites. Thus there were in the whole country one hundred and seventy-four fewer children to each one thousand women among Negroes in 1900 than there were in 1880, and seventy-eight fewer among the whites. It will be seen from this that the decrease is more than twice as great among the former as among the latter. In the South Atlantic division the relative decline in the twenty years has been one hundred and fifty-seven for Negroes and seventy-one for whites, while in the South Central division the figures are one hundred and eighty-seven for Negroes and ninety for whites. From these figures it will be seen that the birth rate of the Negro is declining more rapidly than that of the whites. This fact, together with the higher death rate of Negroes, indicates that the relative increase of the race would necessarily be smaller than that of the whites. The census figures for population prove this to be true.

Possible Explanations.

We have already noted two facts which help to account for the larger increase of whites than Negroes in the South. First is the fact of immigration of Northern whites to the South and the emigration of Negroes out of the South. The second fact was the relative health conditions of the two races among the ever-increasing population in cities. There are three other facts which ought to be taken into consideration in connection with these statistics. The first relates to the relative medical attention and physical care taken of the Negro before and since 1860. During slavery days the health of the Negro was watched very carefully, not only from a humanitarian standpoint, but also from the economic as well.

Whenever a Negro became ill it was the common custom

for the mistress of the home to go personally to the quarters and see that proper care was taken of the patient. Most of the plantation owners had a regular physician whom they paid for practice among their slaves. In this way the health of the Negro was much more carefully guarded than at the present time. The one hopeful feature of the present is in the larger number of negro physicians who will necessarily practice largely among their own race. The white physicians prefer not to do the practice among colored people, and race prejudice has often prevented the white man being called in. The consequence has been the poorest medical attention conceivable for the whole people, thousands dying without ever seeing a doctor at all. Neither has there been any hospital facilities to take the place of the old plantation care. The following statement from a Southern city will indicate the condition:

"Here in this city of push, pluck and Christian progress, there is not a decent hospital where colored people can be cared for. At the Grady Hospital, which takes about $20,000 of the city's money annually to run it, is a small wooden annex down by the kitchen, in which may be crowded fifty or sixty beds, and that is all the hospital advantages 40,000 colored citizens have. But, on the other hand, our whites, with a population of about 70,000, have all the wards and private rooms in the entire brick building at this hospital, together with a very fine hospital here known as St. Joseph's Infirmary."[1]

With the increasing number of medical graduates among Negroes and the larger interest of Southern whites in the Negro, this condition ought to be somewhat changed.

Lack of Care for Children.

Another fact which helps to explain the high death rate and consequent smaller increase of negro population lies

---

[1]"Mortality Among Negroes in Cities," p. 17.

in the poor care taken of the negro children. The census figures for 1900 show that 62.2 per cent of all Negroes over ten years of age are breadwinners, and 46.9 per cent of Southern whites of the same age. Among women 40.7 per cent among Negroes over ten years of age and 11.8 per cent of Southern whites are breadwinners. Perhaps fully 50 per cent of all negro women of motherhood age have to work for a living. This means that most of the children have no adequate care. In a tour of investigation in Columbia, S. C., recently, I found a home of six children where the mother cooked for a white family. She had a three-months-old baby and had been away from it continually during the day hours since the child was one week old. She simply gave it a sugar bag to suck, and, locking the door, left it in the house alone all day, coming home once during the day to nurse it. The other children were away at school or at work. It would be nothing less than a miracle if this child should grow into a healthy youth, and yet this condition is found in nearly half of the negro homes. We berate the negro women for not being more willing to work out, and when they do we accuse them of lack of love for their children, and put down the smaller birth rate and the higher death rate as a matter of race weakness. The real truth is that the infant mortality among city Negroes is so overwhelmingly high as to materially affect the entire rate of population increase. If we want to have negro women to do the work in our homes, common humanity and decency would dictate that we provide day nurseries to guard the children of these women while they cook our meals and nurse our own children. It is also a well-known fact that there are many more stillborn children among the Negroes than among the whites. This is explained partly by the larger exposure of the negro working women and partly by immorality and sexual diseases. In either case it helps to lessen the rate of increase in negro population.

Increase in Special Diseases.

In a former volume I have gone somewhat into detail concerning the increased prevalence of consumption, scrofula, syphilis, etc. I do not need to repeat these statistics here. Without wearying the reader with figures, one can simply summarize conclusions as to causes in so far as the facts make these causes clear. First, much of the consumption is due to exposure, poor sanitation, type of labor done, such as laundering clothes for sick people, and also due to a large debilitation on the part of the Negro on account of sexual immorality. This weakness on the part of the parents gives the child much less resisting power to fight the inroads of this disease. Second, this increased immorality would naturally come along with the first half century of freedom. To almost every ignorant people freedom means license, and this is not always confined to the ignorant people. Also the great preponderance of women among the colored population of the cities (118 women to 100 men in fifteen of the cities of largest negro population) exposes the women of a weak and untrained race to greater temptations than they could be expected to overcome. Still further, the economic pressure and the high cost of living have delayed marriage by a number of months for the whole race in the last twenty years, thus opening a new avenue of immorality. All these facts will help to indicate why these specific diseases have increased since 1860 among Negroes. With a larger moral training which they are now getting in the schools, with better hygienic and sanitary knowledge which the school children are acquiring, and with a more genuine interest and helpfulness on the part of whites, these conditions ought to show a change for the better in the next decade.

Negro Conditions an American Problem.

The foregoing brief summary of vital statistics, together with the succeeding maps showing the present race distribution, lead me to a number of very definite conclusions. The first is that the condition of the Negro, while preponderantly a Southern question, is also fast becoming a national question.

It will be seen from the above that there is a steady flow from the South to the North, and if the South Atlantic States did not include Maryland and Delaware the numbers would be increased by some seven thousand, and a similar decrease in the total in the South for 1910. A careful study of the facts in the South indicates also that the Negroes are becoming more widely spread and somewhat more evenly divided. Only a few counties go contrary to this rule. It is, therefore, evident that every American citizen must become more and more interested in the uplift of this race.

NUMBER OF NEGROES LIVING IN STATES OUTSIDE THE SOUTH

Negro Population	1900	1910
For Continental U. S.	8,833,994	9,828,294
For South Atlantic and South Central	7,922,969	8,247,390
For States Outside the South	911,025	1,078,804

The Negro a Factor in the Future.

While all the facts go to show that the Negro is increasing less rapidly than the white man, nevertheless even the most conservative estimates indicate that for more than a century to come he will be a very large factor in Southern life. We and our children and our children's children will still have the problem of a proper race relationship between two peoples comparatively equal in numbers. It is pure weakness that prompts us to spend time theorizing about the possibility of race extinction. This is not likely to ever come, but if it should ever come it will be many generations removed. Instead of speculating about that probable hour, and wishing that hour to speedily arrive, it would be far more statesmanlike and more human and more Christian if we would begin to do something to uplift those who are with us now. The man who theorizes about race extinction is nine times out of ten doing nothing for race elevation. What we need today is not more theorists, but more workers—more men and women who are willing to do their duty by the people of our own day, and leave the future to God and the workings of the laws of nature.

Country Conditions Most Favorable to the Negro.

Our study further convinces us that the conditions of rural life are much more conducive to the welfare, both physical and moral, of the Negro than the city. For the present, at least, he is not economically fitted in large numbers to be a city dweller. Not only so, but his impulsive nature unfits him to meet the excitement and strain of city life. The one wholesome and safe place for the mass of Negroes is in the country and on the farms. It is to be noted that the negro farmer is increasing somewhat faster than the white farmer in the South. This is not only to the advantage of the Negro, but to the economic advantage of the whole section. The South is an agricultural section, and we must induce the Negro to have his share in the agricultural life of the section if we are to prosper. Some of the things necessary to keep the Negro in the country will be discussed in a later chapter. Here we want to call attention alone to the fact that vital statistics point to the country as the hope of the Negro population.

Self Interest and Negro Population.

The greatest economic need of the present South is an

intelligent and able-bodied laboring class. We have the wealth of soil, the abundance of timber, and mineral resources beyond reasonable measure. These cannot be developed without efficient labor, and lack of this more than anything else is the cause of our backwardness at the present time. No one can go to a cotton plantation today and not hear the cry of scarcity of labor—because we neither have sufficient supply nor is that supply properly trained. The normal, healthy growth of the negro population is, therefore, a thing devoutly to be wished. We cannot prosper without his services, for, as I have pointed out elsewhere, we cannot hope for a very large inflow of labor from the foreign element in the near future. Conditions in the South do not appeal to the foreigner and he prefers to settle in the North and West. If, therefore, we allow careless sanitation in our cities, thereby increasing the death rate among the negro, we do it at our own economic peril. Whether we care for the man or no, we must, as a section, care for the fruit of his labor. A laboring man today is more valuable than he was during slavery. A good hand could then be hired for one hundred and fifty dollars per year and his board. He certainly produces more than that now, and every child which fails to grow into strong manhood simply because of our neglect is robbing the South of that much productive energy.

Our Responsibility.

Furthermore, if the negro race is dying rapidly, the white man is responsible. I mean in the country we give him so little training in the laws of hygiene that he does not know the art of self-preservation. I mean that we allow city landlords to build abominable huts in which the Negro has to live. We allow the streets in the section where he lives—even though within the city limits—to go without drainage, sewerage, paving, or even garbage service. We allow practices which no self-respecting community ought to allow, and all these things result in indifference, immorality, physical inability and death for the Negro—*and we are his murderers.* A city council which allows any land owner to do what I saw done in one Southern city recently— build a long row of shabby houses inside the corporate limits, in a marsh, without drainage or sewerage, putting the houses up on posts to keep them out of the water, and rent those houses at 40 per cent interest on his investment—any city council that will allow this is either a set of civic imbeciles or a set of civic knaves. Nay, more, they are a set of civic murderers. The fact that these men go to church on Sunday and subscribe to the Y. M. C. A. on Monday, and make a civic righteousness speech on Tuesday, and lead the parade for the "City Ad" Club on Wednesday, and so on through the week, does not make them any less criminal. The truth is that in our day the criminal most to be feared is not the red-handed murderer or the pad-footed robber, but the men who, clothed in all their high respectability, sit in their fine offices and smile, while poor devils all around them are dying for want of protection from the greed of the money shark, the lust of the landlord, and the chicanery of the cheap politician. The weeping of this people ascendeth to high heaven, and we raise not our hand to stay the cause of their lamentation. Men of the South, we who glory in the passing of the Negro are glorying because of the red-handed murder done by our own race, and the blood of the sufferers will be on our heads. ,

Law of Retribution.

And already that blood is on our heads. Already the law of retribution has begun to strike back, and whenever a black boy dies of tuberculosis he leaves behind him a train of suffering white boys who have contracted his disease. Wherever a poor, degraded negro girl passes on because of her crimes of life, she leaves some white mother and some white child suffering the pangs of an ever-present death because she has dragged with her some white man to the very jaws of hell. If the figures I have given spell anything, they spell responsibility. Instead of glorying, as some, in what seems to be the decay of the negro race, self-interest, self-instinct, self-preservation, humanity, Christianity—all unite in demanding that we stay this tide of death. The negro race, as we saw in our first chapter, is essentially a prolific race. His nature has not and could not completely change in a brief period of two or three centuries. If he has become or is becoming a waning race, it is not because of inherent racial disability, but because his environment has been unfavorable. And it should be noted that this environment may be changed. There is not a cause working for the more rapid decrease of the negro population which is not curable. If we shall give them more decent homes to live in and more decent surroundings, impurity will be less prevalent and infant mortality reduced. If we shall see to it that they have better sanitation and better training in the laws of hygiene, there will be less of tuberculosis, fevers and death. If we shall encourage them to have better homes and help them to have a larger share in the returns of labor, if we shall cease to exploit them for our own selfish pleasure, they will begin to have more hope, more courage, and hence a better chance for a long and useful life. I cannot but believe that the bare physical life of the Negro is largely in the hands of the white man. We must be true to that trust.

ADDENDA

I am greatly indebted to the Negro Bulletin No. 8 (1904), which anyone can secure from the Census Bureau, for many of the facts contained in this chapter. All the facts available at this date from the 1910 census have been incorporated, and sufficient facts are at hand to indicate clearly the trend of present conditions. I am indebted to Dr. Thomas Jesse Jones, of the Census Bureau, for getting into my hands at a very early date the preliminary census returns (1910) which make possible the maps following and the general statement of facts concerning the population. There may be some slight changes later in the census returns, but they will be so slight as not to affect the value of this work.

In order that one may know at a glance the distribution of negro population, the maps following leave all counties white where the whites have increased more rapidly than the blacks during the decade from 1900 to 1910. When the blacks have increased parallel with or faster than the whites, the counties have been barred. In every case the percentage of increase for each is given. The top figure refers to the whites; the bottom figures to the blacks. A minus sign before a figure indicates a decrease. Thus a county marked (cut in) would mean the whites had increased four per cent and the Negroes had decreased two per cent between 1900 and 1910. Where a single figure is given in a county, it means both races have increased or decreased at the same rate, or at least so nearly the same rate as to make no appreciable difference. It is hoped that these maps may show at a glance the general migrations of Negroes in the former slave-holding States, and hence no extended comments have been made. The appended figures will give more detailed information for each State.

White and Negro Population by Decades from 1890 to 1910, together with Percentage of Negroes to Total Population and Percentage of Negro Increase by Decades.

	1890			1900			1910			Per cent of Negro to Total Pop.		Per cent of Increase in Negro Pop.	
	White	Negro	Others	White	Negro	Others	White	Negro	Others	1900	1910	1890–1900	1900–1910
Georgia	978,357	857,815	181	1,181,294	1,034,813	224	1,431,816	1,176,987	318	46.7	45.1	20.5	13.7
Virginia	1,020,122	635,834	420	1,192,855	660,722	607	1,389,809	671,096	707	35.6	32.6	4.0	1.6
Mississippi ..	544,851	742,559	2,190	641,200	907,630	2,440	786,119	1,009,487	1,508	57.6	56.2	.2	11.2
Arkansas	818,752	309,117	342	944,580	366,856	128	1,131,030	442,891	528	28.0	28.1	15.4	19.7
Alabama	833,718	678,489	1,194	1,001,152	827,307	238	1,228,841	908,275	977	44.8	42.5	219	9.8
N. Carolina..	1,055,382	561,018	1,549	1,263,603	624,469	5,738	1,500,513	697,843	7,931	33.0	31.6	11.3	11.7
Louisiana	558,395	559,193	1,00	729,612	650,804	1,209	941,125	713,874	1,389	42.1	43.1	16.4	9.7
W. Virginia ..	730,077	32,690	27	915,233	43,499	68	1,156,817	64,173	129	4.5	5.3	33.1	47.5
Kentucky	1,590,462	268,071	102	1,862,309	284,706	159	2,027,955	261,636	294	13.3	11.4	6.2	-8.1
S. Carolina ..	462,008	688,934	207	537,807	782,321	188	679,162	835,843	395	59.1	55.2	13.7	6.8
Tennessee ..	1,336,637	403,151	146	1,540,186	480,243	108	1,711,550	472,997	252	23.7	21.1	5.6	-1.5
Florida	224,949	166,180	293	297,333	230,730	479	443,646	308,669	304	43.7	41.0	38.8	33.8
Texas	1,745,935	488,171	1,421	2,426,669	620,722	1,319	3,204,896	690,020	1,626	20.4	17.7	27.2	11.2
Maryland	826,943	215,657	240	952,424	235,064	556	1,062,645	232,249	452	19.8	17.9	9.0	-1.2
Delaware	140,066	28,386	41	153,977	30,697	61	171,103	30,181	38	16.8	15.4	8.1	1.8
Oklahoma	172,554	21,609	64,494	670,204	55,684	64,503	1,444,535	137,612	75,008	7.0	8.3	157.7	147.1

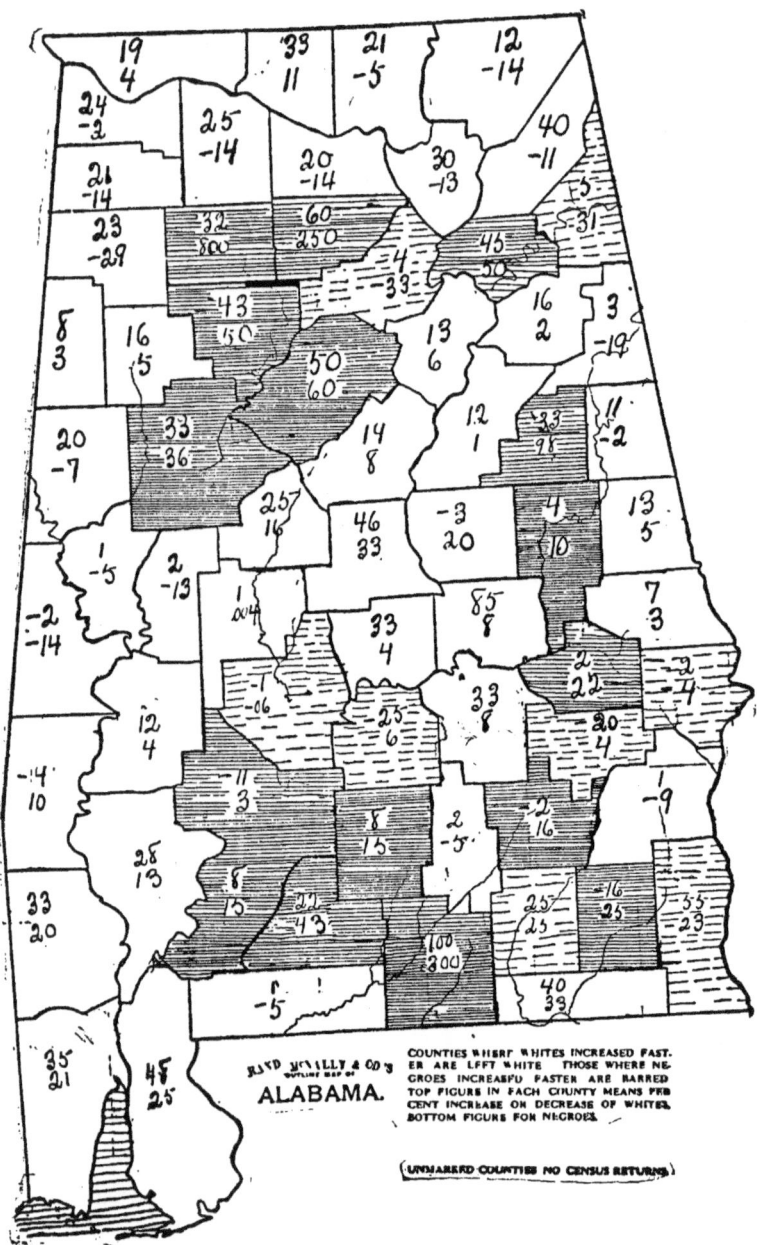

COUNTIES WHERE WHITES INCREASED FASTER ARE LEFT WHITE. THOSE WHERE NEGROES INCREASED FASTER ARE BARRED. TOP FIGURES IN EACH COUNTY MEANS PER CENT INCREASE OR DECREASE OF WHITES, BOTTOM FIGURES FOR NEGROES.

RAND McNALLY & CO'S
OUTLINE MAP OF
ALABAMA.

(UNMARKED COUNTIES NO CENSUS RETURNS.)

ARKANSAS.

RAND, McNALLY & CO.'S
OUTLINE MAP OF
ARKANSAS.

COUNTIES WHERE WHITES INCREASED FAST-
ER ARE LEFT WHITE, THOSE WHERE NE-
GROES INCREASED FASTER ARE BARRED.
TOP FIGURE IN EACH COUNTY MEANS PER
CENT INCREASE OR DECREASE OF WHITES.
BOTTOM FIGURE FOR NEGROES.

UNMARKED COUNTIES NO CENSUS RETURNS.

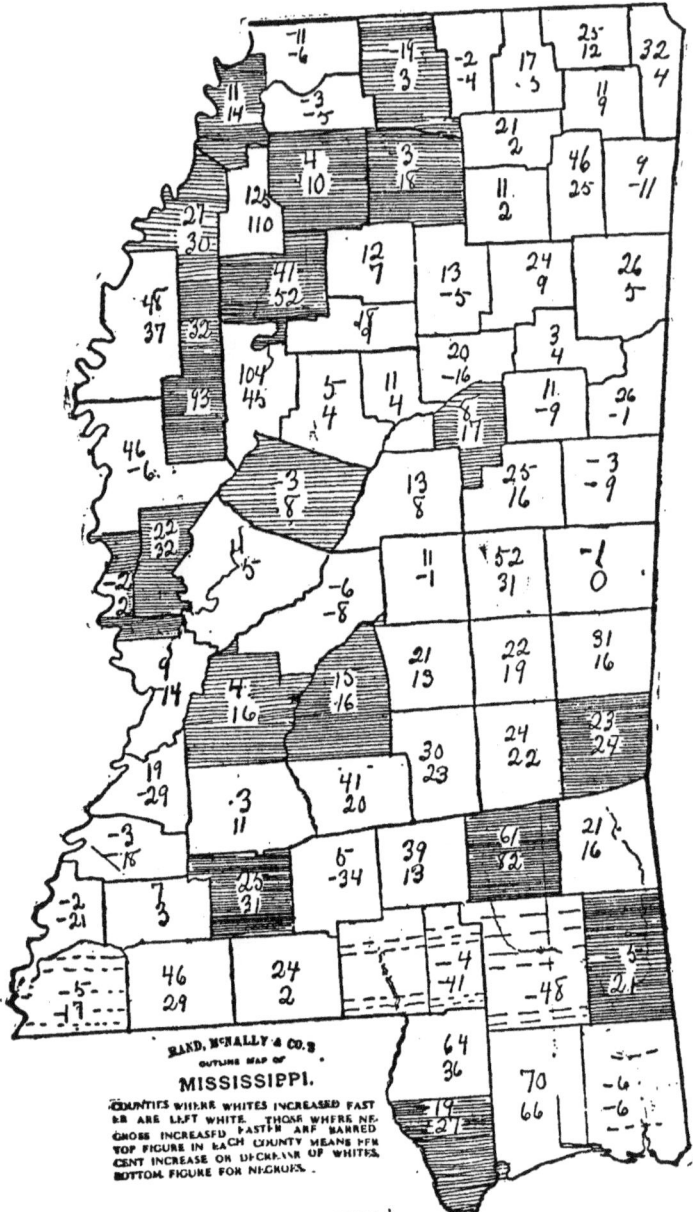

RAND, McNALLY & CO.'S
OUTLINE MAP OF
MISSISSIPPI.

COUNTIES WHERE WHITES INCREASED FAST
OR ARE LEFT WHITE. THOSE WHERE NE-
GROES INCREASED FASTER ARE BARRED
TOP FIGURE IN EACH COUNTY MEANS PER
CENT INCREASE OR DECREASE OF WHITES,
BOTTOM FIGURE FOR NEGROES.

UNMARKED COUNTIES NO CENSUS RETURNS.

RAND, McNALLY & CO.
OUTLINE MAP OF
GEORGIA.

COUNTIES WHERE WHITES INCREASED FAST-
ER ARE LEFT WHITE. THOSE WHERE NE-
GROES INCREASED FASTER ARE BARRED.
TOP FIGURE IN EACH COUNTY MEANS PER
CENT INCREASE OR DECREASE OF WHITES,
BOTTOM FIGURE FOR NEGROES.

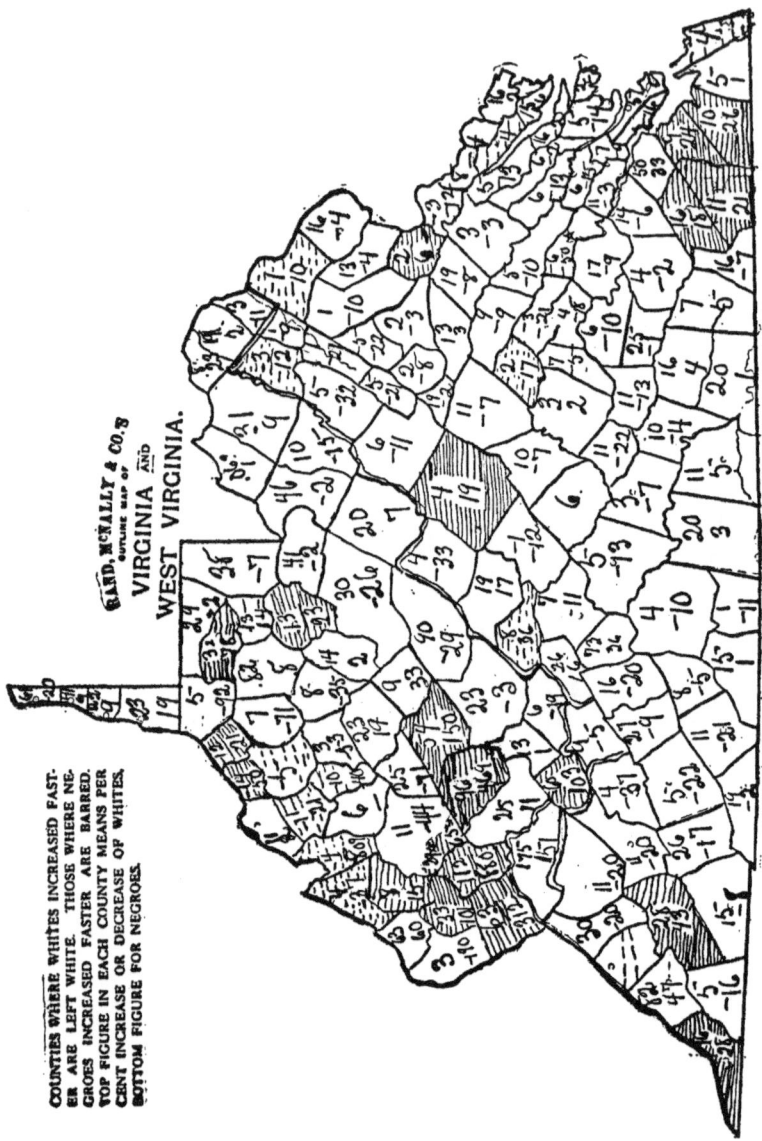

COUNTIES WHERE WHITES INCREASED FAST-
ER ARE LEFT WHITE. THOSE WHERE NE-
GROES INCREASED FASTER ARE BARRED.
TOP FIGURE IN EACH COUNTY MEANS PER
CENT INCREASE OR DECREASE OF WHITES.
BOTTOM FIGURE FOR NEGROES.

RAND, McNALLY & CO.'S
OUTLINE MAP OF
VIRGINIA AND
WEST VIRGINIA.

UNIV. OF
CALIFORNIA

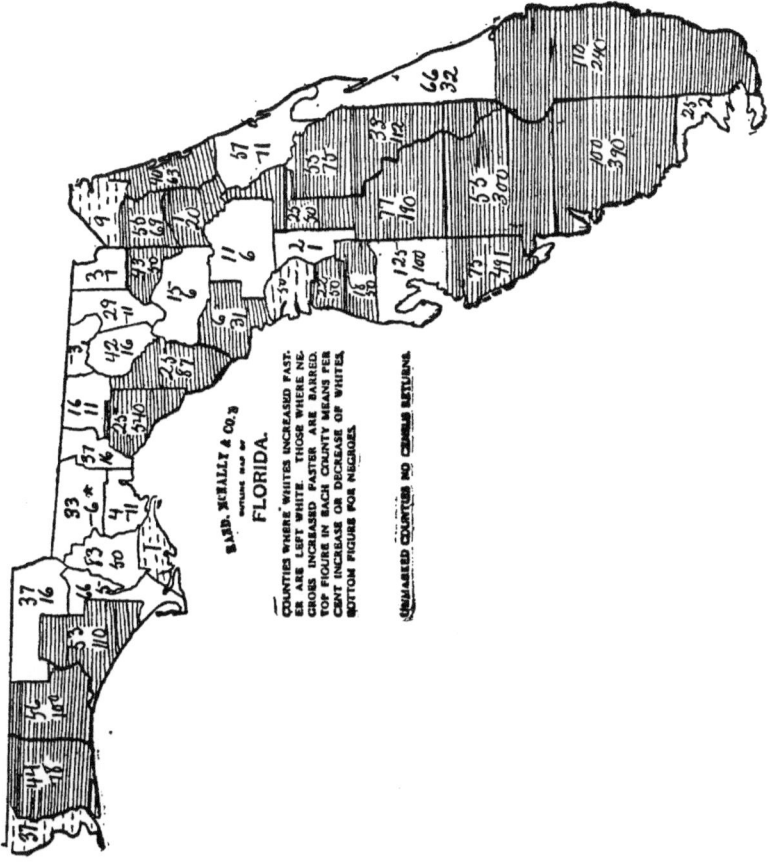

RAND, McNALLY & CO.'S
MAP OF
FLORIDA.

COUNTIES WHERE WHITES INCREASED FAST-
ER ARE LEFT WHITE. THOSE WHERE NE-
GROS INCREASED FASTER ARE BARRED.
TOP FIGURE IN EACH COUNTY MEANS PER
CENT INCREASE OR DECREASE OF WHITES.
BOTTOM FIGURE FOR NEGROES.

UNMARKED COUNTIES NO CENSUS RETURNS.

RAND, McNALLY & CO.'S
Outline Map of
OKLAHOMA
AND
INDIAN TERRITORY.

COUNTIES WHERE WHITES INCREASED FAST-
ER ARE LEFT WHITE. THOSE WHERE NE-
GROES INCREASED FASTER ARE BARRED.
TOP FIGURE IN EACH COUNTY MEANS PER
CENT INCREASE OR DECREASE OF WHITES,
BOTTOM FIGURE FOR NEGROES.

UNMARKED COUNTIES NO CENSUS RETURNS.

RAND M?NALLY & CO.'S
SECTION MAP OF
LOUISIANA

COUNTIES WHERE WHITES INCREASED FAST-
ER ARE LEFT WHITE. THOSE WHERE NE-
GROES INCREASED FASTER ARE BARRED.
TOP FIGURE IN EACH COUNTY MEANS PER
CENT INCREASE OR DECREASE OF WHITES.
BOTTOM FIGURE FOR NEGROES.

(UNMARKED COUNTIES NO CENSUS RETURNS)

COUNTIES WHERE WHITES INCREASED FAST-
ER ARE LEFT WHITE, THOSE WHERE NE-
GROES INCREASED FASTER ARE BARRED
TOP FIGURE IN EACH COUNTY MEANS PER
CENT INCREASE OR DECREASE OF WHITES
BOTTOM FIGURE FOR NEGROES

UNMARKED COUNTIES NO CENSUS RETURNS

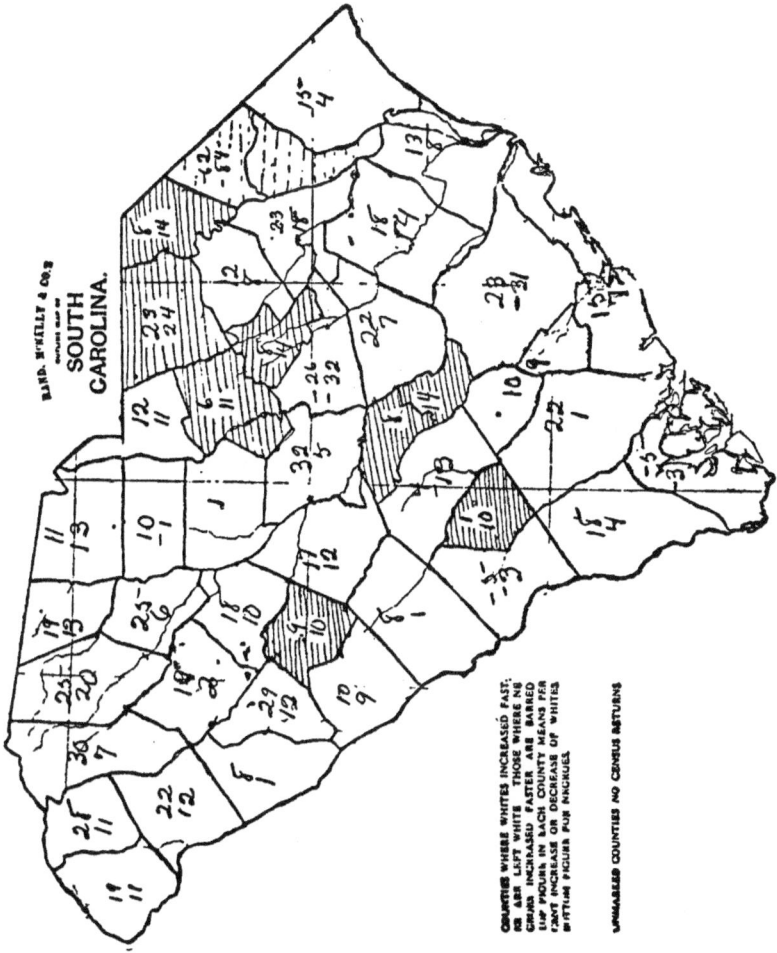

RAND. M^cNALLY & CO.'S

**SOUTH
CAROLINA.**

COUNTIES WHERE WHITES INCREASED FAST;
63 ARE LEFT WHITE; THOSE WHERE NE-
GROES INCREASED FASTER ARE BARRED
UP. FIGURE IN EACH COUNTY MEANS PER
CENT INCREASE OR DECREASE OF WHITES.
BOTTOM FIGURE FOR NEGROES.

UNMARKED COUNTIES NO CENSUS RETURNS

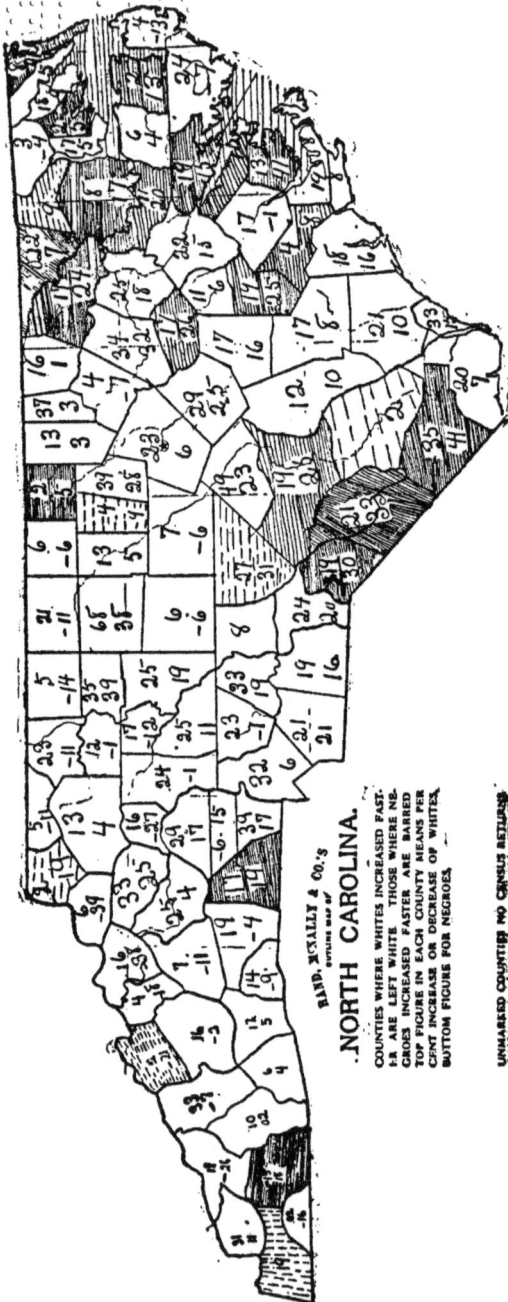

RAND, McNALLY & CO.'S
OUTLINE MAP OF
NORTH CAROLINA.

COUNTIES WHERE WHITES INCREASED FAST-
ER ARE LEFT WHITE. THOSE WHERE NE-
GROES INCREASED FASTER ARE BARRED.
TOP FIGURE IN EACH COUNTY MEANS PER
CENT INCREASE OR DECREASE OF WHITES,
BOTTOM FIGURE FOR NEGROES.

UNBARRED COUNTIES NO CENSUS RETURNS

RAND McNALLY & Co.'s
OUTLINE MAP OF
MARYLAND AND
DELAWARE

COUNTIES WHERE WHITES INCREASED FAST-
ER ARE LEFT WHITE. THOSE WHERE NE-
GROES INCREASED FASTER ARE BARRED.
TOP FIGURE IN EACH COUNTY MEANS PER
CENT INCREASE OR DECREASE OF WHITES.
BOTTOM FIGURE FOR NEGROES.

UNMARKED COUNTIES NO CENSUS RETURNS

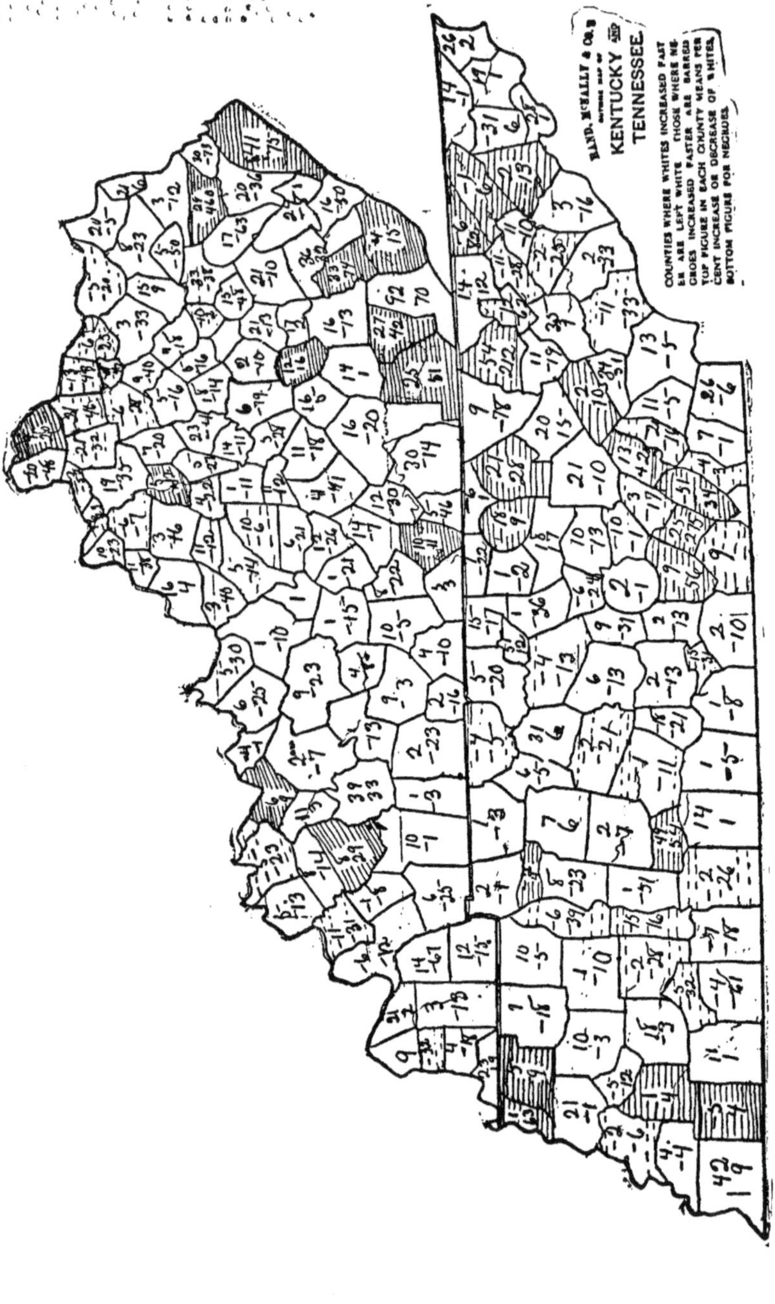

CHAPTER IV

THE NEW TYPE OF NEGRO FARMER

A CORN SONG

O'er the fields with heavy tread,
Light of heart and high of head,
Though the halting steps be labored, slow, and weary;
Still the spirits brave and strong
Find a comforter in song,
And their corn-song rises ever loud and cheery.
Oh, we hoe de co'n
Since de ehly mo'n;
Now de sinkin' sun
Says de day is done.

—Paul Laurence Dunbar.

CHAPTER IV

THE NEW TYPE OF NEGRO FARMER

There is a glory about the old Southern life which holds one like an enchantment. Here and there, as one travels over this section, one still stumbles upon these old plantations, the ruins of which yet stand, publishing to the world the glories of a past, but not a forgotten age. Here will be seen a long line of cedars or elms or maples, flanking a winding roadway that leads back to some secluded spot where stood the manor of a Southern gentleman. These old trees, standing as lonely but faithful sentinels guarding the remains of a past glory, seem to have about them some of the former dignity and pride of bearing which characterized those who drove beneath their shades. But with all their dignity there lingers about them an inviting atmosphere and a comfortable leisure which reminds one of the genial hospitality of the typical Southern home of half a century ago.

If one has chanced upon one of the best preserved of these old places, there can still be seen standing the neighborly little houses of the slave quarters, all huddled together in that friendly familiarity which characterizes the people sprung from their simple hearths. Here and there smoke will be rising from the dilapidated chimney of one of the rickety huts, and if one lingers long enough a frosty-haired old Negro will put his head out at the door and give you one of those cordial and kindly greetings which transports you into another time.

Here are the stables, now decaying and empty, in which the prancing steeds were fondled and petted by that proud coachman whose face shone as brightly as his carriage, and whose head was held no less proudly than that of the dashing team. All about you there are signs of a former prosperity, and a rich glory which no Southern man can ever forget, and which no true Southerner would want to forget. I frankly confess, call it sentiment if you will, that I never visit one of these Southern plantations, where peace and chivalry were wont to dwell, that the blood in my veins does not leap faster, and there is not an almost irresistible impulse to go with uncovered head and to say to those about me, "Take off thy shoes, for the ground where on thou standest is sacred ground."

But with all the glory of its past, the regime of slave farming was a failure. It was built upon the false principle of great landed estates on which the few had luxury and the mass had only a living. The conditions of slave labor drove the South deeper and deeper into that profligate method of farming which plants only one crop and continues to mine and dig until all the strength of the land has been extracted, and then, like a tired man, the land, exhausted and lean, must lie and rest for a century before nature can so far resuscitate it as to make it able to take up the burden of crop-raising again.

The following excerpt taken from the report of the Wateree Agricultural Society, of South Carolina, 1843, while declaiming for better farming methods, clearly indicates the process of land destruction during slavery.

"For many years, while our chief marketable product, cotton, bore a high price, many of us were in the habit of raising that almost exclusively, and depending upon supplies of bread and meat from abroad, which the cotton crop had to pay for—as well as for the animal power necessary on the plantation; a most pernicious practice, which has impoverished the State by millions, and been the ruin of many planters. It is believed that stern necessity has forced the planter to abandon this system measurably. It is unusual for any one in this neighborhood to purchase either bread or meat, and we are rapidly becoming raisers of our own animal power on the plantations.

"It is believed that we are as successful as any body of planters in the State, on the same character of lands, in the mode of our culture. *Certainly we have pressed too far the old, and seemingly well-established doctrine, to wear out the land by cropping without manure, and then open new lands.* But this system is also giving way to the sober light of experience; which teaches, that one acre well manured and taken care of, will produce more in the average of years, than two acres even of fresh land, not manured."[1]

In letters from John B. Lamar to Mrs. Howell Cobb, his sister, and Mr. Howell Cobb, whose plantations, in Georgia, he managed, I take extracts showing the same conditions of worn-out land.

". . . Lord, Lord Howell, you and I have been too used to poor land to know what crops people are making in the rich lands of the new counties. I am just getting my eyes opened to the golden view. On those good lands, when cotton is down to such a price as would starve us out, they can make money. . . . You have a large and effective force of hands, more effective than any of the same number I know of in the States. But they cultivate a large proportion of poor land, and there is not enough of even poor land in Baldwin for them to be properly employed. . . . I have been asleep to my interests for ten years. I have just woke up from a Rip Van Winkle nap and found everybody around me advancing and I just holding my own on poor lands that were (most of them) exhausted before I ever saw them."[2]

It was inevitable that the old method of big farms, slave

---

[1] Quoted from Documentary History of American Industrial Society, pp. 290, 291.

[2] *Ibid*, pp. 177, 178, 179.

hands and paid overseers should have just this result. Every overseer wanted to make the largest possible show for the year at the least possible expense, and the result was that everything was taken off the land and nothing put back. The wonder is that more lands were not destroyed than were.

Amount Cultivated.

Mr. John Lee Coulter, of the Department of Commerce and Labor, has prepared a statement concerning farm life in the Southern States east of the Mississippi River, a copy of which manuscript he has been kind enough to put into my hands. According to his estimate there were farms in these States aggregating 161,607,000 acres in 1860, and these farms contained on an average 321 acres. The number of farms was 504,000, and the land, building improvement and machinery were all valued at $2,048,000,000. The immediate effect of the war was to throw much of this land out of cultivation because of lack of labor and lack of capital, and reduce farm values to half the former amount. In 1870 the total farm values listed were $1,137,000,000, in 1880 it was $1,486,000,000, in 1890 it was $1,875,000,000, and not till 1900 did it stand at $2,135,000,000, just 4 per cent more than it was reported in 1860. These figures tell a long story of painful toil and slow, patient recovery. None who failed to see the two types of life can ever know quite what the war really cost the South. While the remainder of the country was forging ahead, forty years were consumed in the South getting back to where we were in 1860. It is with gladness and hope that we report a growth of 102 per cent in farm values from 1900 to 1910, the figures now standing at $4,318,000,000.

Smaller Farms.

The amount of land in farms in these Southeastern

States in 1910 (163,000,000 acres) is only a comparatively
few acres more than in 1860, and yet there are four times
as many farms now as then, making the average size of a
farm today only 84 acres, about half of which is in cultivation, the other half being in woods lot, pasture, etc.
This marks a long step in the progress of the South, for it
' means more independent farmers and better cultivated
farms. The number of white farmers in the United States
in 1910 was 5,422,892, an increase of 9.1 per cent over the
previous decade, while the number of colored farms was
917,465, or an increase of 19.5 per cent. Thus it seems
the Negro has a greater disposition to stay on the farm than
has the white man.

Enemies of Southern Farm Life.

The three arch enemies of Southern farm life today are
the tenant system, which appears under various guises; the
one crop system, which continues to do what it did during
slavery—eat up the land and leave it worthless; and lastly,
that form of isolation which cheats the rural dweller out
of his birthright of culture, growth and enjoyment. All of
those evils bear more heavily on the average Negro than on
the white man in the country.

The Tenant System.

Before the war the large farms in the South were
worked by gangs of slaves usually under the eye of an
overseer, while the smaller farms in the North were worked
by hired labor. After the war the old plantation owner
began to divide his farm up into smaller plots and rent each
plot to a family for cultivation. He had no other recourse,
for he did not have enough surplus cash to hire labor to do
the work, and besides, hired labor was very unreliable and
scarcely to be had. Many of the old slaves stayed on the
plantation and the owner aided them to the best of his

ability by standing for their credit at the store where they got provisions and seed to carry them until the crop could be made. In this way there gradually grew up in the South a tenant system. The terms of tenantry are of three kinds: First, a cash tenant or renter; second, one who pays a fixed amount of produce; and third, the sharer or cropper who pays one-half or one-fourth of what he makes in accordance with whether or not the landlord furnishes stock and seed, or whether these are furnished by the cropper. The grades of a negro farmer, therefore, are considered to stand in the following order: (1) Owner, (2) cash renter, (3) fourth cropper, (4) half cropper. Many of the Negroes begin at No. 4 and go toward No. 1 as rapidly as possible. The number of farms worked by tenants throughout the United States in 1910 was 2,349,254, or 37.1 per cent of all farms, an increase of 2 per cent over 1900. In Mississippi 66 per cent of the farms are worked by tenants, likewise nearly 66 per cent in Georgia, 63 per cent in South Carolina, 60 per cent in Alabama, 40 per cent in North Carolina and Tennessee, in Kentucky 24 per cent and in Virginia 27 per cent. It will be noted that those States—Mississippi, Georgia and South Carolina—where the negro population is very large are the States where the tenantry system is most prevalent. Therefore, it is seen at once that the Negro is the greatest sufferer from this type of farming. This problem demands careful thought.

More Produce Raised Under the Tenant System.

The old tenant system has been defended times without number by farmers who claim that a Negro, and even the renting whites, can raise more than they would if they owned the land and were free to cultivate it as they pleased. This argument is made on the assumption, true indeed at present, that the mass of these farmers have not sufficient knowledge or persistence to make a good crop without careful supervision. In the tenant system the landlord not only stipulates what shall be planted, when and where it shall be planted, but he usually keeps an eye on the growing crop and sees to it that the tenant keeps it worked and gathers it properly. There can be no doubt that this does help to increase the yield with all the less experienced and less ambitious farmers. But it is not alone what a man makes that benefits him, it is what he lays away or wisely spends. In the figures gathered by the 1910 census it has come out quite clearly that while á share tenant actually produces more on the average than a cash tenant or an owner, yet the cash tenant saves more and has more to show for his labor than the cropper, and the owner has more to show than the cash tenant. From the standpoint, therefore, of the farmer we must, of necessity, favor the small farm ownership among Negroes as well as whites. We can only hope that more careful training and continued responsibility will enable them to raise as much as they would under white supervision.

One-Crop System and Tenantry.

It ought also to be mentioned that where the one crop system prevails, that is, where only cotton, tobacco or sugar cane is raised, the farms tend to increase in size and all the land tends to be cultivated by the cropper. Thus in the Mississippi and Brazos River bottoms, one can easily see thousands of acres cultivated under one management, every Negro having a little plot which he farms, paying one-fourth of his produce for the use of the land. I drove one day in the Brazos bottom through plantations measuring 1,900 acres, 2,400 acres, 2,900 acres, 5,000 acres and 10,000 acres, respectively, and in all my drive saw only one plot of land that belonged to a Negro. On all these plantations cotton alone was raised, with just enough corn to feed the mules and horses, often not that much.

Here the tenant starts the year in debt, so he must go to the landlord's store and get provisions and supplies on credit. Usually he is allowed ten to twelve dollars per month for supplies, and a little money to buy whisky on Saturday. When the crop is gathered in the fall there is comparatively little left after the bill at the store has been paid. In many cases the Negro is charged two prices for his supplies, and if it looks as though the crop would be extra good, he is encouraged to spend more liberally. Not a few planters keep the Negro perpetually in debt in order that it may be impossible for him to move off the place at the close of the year.

Tenantry and Whiskey.

One of the paradoxes I have met in traveling through these tenant-farming districts is the attitude of the manager toward whiskey and the Negro. If you sit down to discuss with him the economic efficiency of the Negro, he will usually swear at him, call him worthless, unambitious, shiftless and almost anything vile. He never fails to tell you that the Negro will not work Saturday, for that is his day for drinking and gambling, which carousal lasts into Sunday, and then most of Monday must be used in "sobering up." I had one planter tell me in hard earnest he could not get more than three and a half to four days' work out of his tenants—Tuesday morning until Friday noon or Friday night at most. The other three days he said were used in drinking, gambling, carousing and getting sober. When I asked him where they got the whiskey, he said at the plantation store. On my asking why he did not quit selling whiskey, he replied he did not dare, for the Negroes would go to the next plantation and not only buy their whiskey, but spend all their surplus cash. Then I asked why all the planters did not combine and agree to put out whiskey, and his reply was that the Negroes would leave the country. But they had never tried it, and those counties that have tried it have lost absolutely nothing but the worthless class, those whom everybody could well spare.

No, this was not the secret. When I went over to the store I found the real secret. The keeper told me whiskey was his big trade, and the store looked it. There were forty big empty whiskey barrels sitting out on the front platform at that minute. I got a picture of those barrels, though the keeper thought I was taking a picture of his store front. He told me he sold from six to twelve carloads of whiskey per year, and it was cheap whiskey, not cheap to the Negro, but cheap to the store man. The real reason the whiskey stays there is, that the average planter of this type prefers to get, as rent, one-fourth of what a Negro can make working four days in the week; and then get for whiskey nine-tenths of the remaining three-fourths. At the end of the year the poor Negro has drunk up all his surplus and cannot possibly pay out, so he must stick to the land.

Exceptional Landlords.

Of course there are notable exceptions. I have seen many good planters who honestly did their best to help the tenants save and prosper. I visited such a place owned and operated by Mr. R. K. Boney in the Mississippi bottom. He has seventy-five families on his place. The houses are all in good repair. Every family has space for a garden, a yard, pigs, and horses, and cattle. They are encouraged to raise all their meat at home. They are urged to have a garden and to raise enough corn to give them their meal as well as feed. While at Mr. Boney's place he called his Negroes together for me to speak to them on better farming, and at that meeting offered to give them liberal first, second and third money prizes for the most improvement during the year. There are others like Mr. Boney and in them there is much hope for the negro race.

Better Tenants.

Likewise there are exceptions among tenants. Here and there one finds a tenant who will not drink, who saves his money and who means later to buy land. I found one such on the Brazos River, Texas, who after paying all his bills for the year put three thousand dollars in the bank as the result of his year's labor. Another one on the same plantation started without a dollar in money and five hundred dollars in debt. He bought two yoke of oxen with which he made his crop, and when the year closed, after paying for his oxen and settling his debts, he put eight hundred dollars in the bank. But these are the rare exceptions. Most Negroes have not the self-denial to do a thing of this kind, under the existing circumstances.

I believe if the plantations in the South are ever to come to their best producing efficiency, it must be not through the exploitation of the tenant, but through giving him the largest possible share in the fruits of his labor and encouraging him to save the same, thus becoming a more responsible and respectable citizen. The one sure escape from the evils of the tenant system is to help the Negro buy land and to farm for himself.

The One-Crop System.

I have said the one crop system means larger farms and tenantry. It also means a very rapid deterioration of the soil. As one rides through Georgia, South Carolina or Virginia, he sees literally thousands of acres of worn-out land from which all the fertility has been taken, and it has been turned out as worthless. This is due to the continual rotation of a single crop, like cotton, corn or tobacco.

But the wearing out of the soil is not the only evil of the one crop system. It means poverty and lack of home comfort. The man who plants all his field in cotton must spend most of his ready cash for meat and cornmeal; while if he had planted only a part of his field in corn he might have a few good hogs, a garden, some chickens and his own meal right at home, and whatever ready cash his cotton brought might be spent in comforts or simple luxuries.

Thus on St. Helena Island one of the managers of the stores told me that the 7,000 Negroes on the island bought at least three-fourths of all the meat they ate, and bought large quantities of grits (ground corn), both of which they might easily have raised at home. Speaking of the evils of the tenant system, in its relation to soil deterioration, Prof. Carl Kelsey says:

". . . This system has hindered the development of diversified farming, which today is one of the greatest needs of the South. The advances (by the landlord) have been conditioned upon the planting and cultivating a given amount of cotton. . . . All else has faded into insignificance before the necessity of raising cotton. The result on the fertility of the soil is also evident. Luckily cotton makes light demands on the land, but the thin soil of many districts has been unable to stand even the light demands. Guano came just in time, and the later commercial fertilizers have postponed the evil day. The development of the cotton mills has also served to give a local market, which has stimulated the production of cotton. It seems rather evident, however, that the increasing development of western lands will put a heavier burden upon the Atlantic slope. This, of course, will not effect the culture of sea island cotton, which is grown in only limited areas. To meet this handicap a more diversified agriculture must gradually supplant in some way the present over-attention to cotton. In early days Virginia raised much cotton, now it stands toward the bottom of the cotton States. Perhaps it is safe to say that Virginia land has been as much injured by the more exhaustive crop, tobacco, as the other States by cotton. Large areas have been allowed to go back to the woods and local conditions have greatly changed. *How this diversi-fication is to be brought about for the negro is one of the most important questions."*

Country Life and Isolation.

One of the most serious problems of country life, and perhaps the one more difficult to meet than any other, is that of isolation. One prime difference between city life and country life lies in the fact that in the former one continually touches elbows with many others engaged in similar pursuits. Out of this social contact comes contagion of character and inspiration and stimulus for high endeavor. Reading will not take the place of this personal association. But it is just this lack of social contact which makes the most serious handicap to progress in the country. Families are scattered, particularly in the South, where population is sparse, and there is little of community life. The woman especially is at home all day alone, and the man not infrequently works by himself in the field. Here is a special handicap for the negro farmer. He is gregarious and does his best work in a group where all move to the monotonous sound of an oft-repeated refrain. Besides the bleakness and barrenness of the country home, the school and church of the Negro are enough to send cold chills through one's whole system. I have been in close correspondence with the United States farm demonstrators over the South. I have before me full reports from almost all of them, in which they say, almost to a man, that the rural Negro has no form of recreation or amusement. A few say the men go to town for recreation. There are no places of recreation where people gather to meet each other. How to overcome these baneful influences and keep the country people satisfied with the country is the herculean task of our present day.

This perhaps can best be done by setting up better methods of communication by way of rural mail, rural telephone, and better roads. Many a county would find it a paying investment to vote heavy bonds for good country roads, even though a large proportion of the taxes fell on the city, because it would give a more prosperous and contented country life, and in its final analysis few Southern counties are wholly prosperous save in so far as the agricultural pursuits are in a flourishing condition.

Make Schools Attractive.

Furthermore, we must do more to make the country school attractive, and make it more of a community center. I do not know anything more dreary than a little frame school-house, unpainted, set in a small stumpy piece of ground, with the weeds growing rank about it, and surrounded by an atmosphere of disuse and decay. This is poor economy. This little house should be neat and well painted, the grounds should be well kept, flowers should be blooming much of the year, it should have an air of prosperity and cheer about it. Then it should be opened once a week at least for some form of entertainment. There should be spelling bees, moving pictures, social evenings, farmers' meetings, mothers' clubs, boys' debates, sewing circles and what not, held in this little building. In other words, it should act as the social center and clearing house of the community. It is set there not simply as a place for teaching children their a-b, ab's, but as a place to teach the whole community how to live. As I have remarked in another place, the school grounds ought to be the playground of the whole community. Now compare this ideal with what actually exists in any colored community you know! How that old house shrivels and dwarfs in the presence of a picture of what it might be. When we get a sufficient number of county superintendents who really care for the rural school community, both white and colored, we will be on the road toward this larger ideal. In like manner, more must be done with and for the country church. We need a new type of minister who is trained for his place in the country. The old ideal that the country church is a place to forsake as soon as a city appointment can be secured is certainly false. There is no greater chance in the world than to be the pastor and leader of the religious life of a whole country community. There the pastor has little competition for the attention of the people. If he is awake and vital, he can do what he will.

Functions of the Church.

President Butterfield, speaking of the mission of the church to the rural community, puts it thus:[1]

-    "Libraries have been written in support of the thesis that human character finds its heights only under the inspiration and guidance of the religious motive. There is no need of extended argument here. I wish to say squarely, however, *that we cannot, in my judgment, hope adequately to idealize country life nor to secure the largest development either of personal character or of neighborhood welfare, except by appealing to the great Christian principles of the Fatherhood of God, the Masterhood of Jesus and the Brotherhood of Man.*

"This statement is sufficient to justify the church in standing specifically for the maintenance and enlargement of rural ideals, because the Christian church has been for centuries the institution through which these great principles have found voice. The church has a right, therefore, to assume leadership in the permanent work of developing and applying the religious motive to the hopes and aspirations of men. This leadership just now is peculiarly imperative because of the *marked tendency everywhere to reduce our higher life to an unreligious basis.*"

---

[1]"The Country Church and the Rural Problem," p. 80.

The whole of country life needs to be socialized, and better means of communication, better schools, better churches and a larger community spirit will help to do this.

Farm Ownership.

The first mark of real encouragement lies in the fact of increased farm ownership among Negroes. Unfortunately until 1900, the census figures do not discriminate between white and colored ownership. At that time one-third of all the farms in Southern States east of the Mississippi were operated by colored farmers, but only one-fifth of these men owned the farms they operated. The number of owners has greatly increased during the last decade, there being 23,822 more negro farm owners in this section in 1910 than there were in 1900. In some sections of the South ownership has increased much more rapidly than in other sections. In Georgia ownership has increased 28 per cent during the decade, in Virginia 21, while in South Carolina it has increased only 7 per cent.

Thus in Virginia the Negroes now own 1,551,435 acres, valued at $13,517,807. There are in Virginia about four million acres in cultivation, and while the Negroes only own about 6 per cent of the land of the State, it is perfectly safe to say they own from one-eighth to one-tenth of all the land in cultivation. A large proportion of the land which they own is in very small tracts of from five to twenty-five acres, and hence is largely in cultivation. In Gloucester County, Virginia, alone, the Negroes own 1,857 farm plots, assessed at $119,381. These farm plots contain 133,549 acres of land, being 14.79 per cent of the entire acreage of the county.

In visiting St. Helena Island I found that almost every Negro owned his land—usually from ten to twenty-five acres. In one county in Georgia negro farm ownership increased 73 per cent between 1900 and 1910. Reports from the United

States Farm Demonstrators all over the South indicate that Negroes almost everywhere are buying land. To my surprise, of all these men answering my question, as to whether there was any opposition to the Negroes buying land, every man without exception said there was absolutely no opposition.

Farm ownership almost always means better farm methods, greater soil preservation, better farm buildings and equipment, and, what is more important than all, better satisfied farmers, hence better citizens. It also offers opportunity to give the children better training, for the child stays in the same school for a number of years and hence does not lose its grading from year to year. Of all the white farm demonstrators who answered my letters, I think only two questioned whether farm ownership made better farmers of negro men, and no one thought he was a poorer farmer because of ownership.

Heroic Fight of Negroes for Ownership.

The heroic fight which many an obscure negro farmer is making in order to buy his land is splendid beyond the belief of the average white man. I was driving in Nottoway County, Virginia, and came upon a place owned by a Negro named Moses Fitzgerald. I went out into the field where he was at work, and found him barefooted harrowing and sowing clover. I learned something of his simple life story. Born a slave, starting with nothing, he began as a boy to trap rabbits and sell them for fifteen cents each and the hides for three cents each. In this way he accumulated enough to buy his first little plot, on which he began farming; saving scrupulously every penny, until now he owns one hundred and fifty-five acres, has built a good five-room house, has a good team, and sends his children to school.

Another man in the same county interested me very much. Both he and his wife were born slaves. He began buying his little plot shortly after the war, when land was cheap. The piece he bought was badly run down; so he went out on the public road each morning at daylight with a wheelbarrow and shovel and picked up the fertilizer to be placed on his little plot. He now owns one hundred acres of land, has a new house of five rooms, neatly furnished and spotlessly clean, flowers in the yard, and good chickens, hogs, garden, and all the comforts one would expect in a good country home. I could give literally dozens of cases which have come under my personal observation, showing the splendid heroism of these people. They richly deserve to succeed, and this is worth knowing among city people, for we are all too apt to judge the whole negro race by the lazy, shiftless loafer that hangs around the alleys.

Farm Demonstration Work.

If one wants to see an economic regeneration where the economically dead are raised to life, the lepers are cleansed and the blind have their sight restored, he could do no better than to visit some of the work of the United States farm demonstrators in the South. Some of the things we see with our own eyes are more wonderful than the fairy stories with which our mothers charmed away our childish cares.

A farm demonstrator is usually a practical farmer who has had some special training in scientific methods of farming and has proven his ability to make crops. Such a man is employed by the United States Department of Agriculture to study the conditions of his county or district with a view to improvement of soil, adaptation of fertilizers, and choosing of seeds, etc. This demonstrator works by getting a number of individual farmers to agree to cultivate a small plot—usually from one to five acres—under his direction. He prescribes the kind of fertilizer, the method of cultivation and the variety of seed. These government agents are working now in every State in the South, though as yet many counties in each State are untouched. There are both white and colored demonstrators, but in counties where there are no colored demonstrators, the white men often help the negro farmers just as they do the white farmers. *I am sorry to say this is not always the case.*

Alabama Demonstration Work.

Just what this method of work is accomplishing will be readily seen from the report of Mr. B. L. Moss, State Agent for Alabama:[1]

"Reports received to date from our agents indicate that they had an average of thirty demonstrations in cotton, averaging three acres each, or a total of ninety acres of cotton per agent worked according to demonstration methods. The same reports indicate that they had an average of twenty corn demonstrations each, averaging two and one-half acres, or a total of fifty acres of corn per agent working according to demonstration methods. Multiplying these figures by seventy, the number of agents employed in Alabama, we have a total of 3,600 acres of cotton and 3,500 acres of corn worked according to demonstration methods. The average yield per acre on these cotton demonstrations will certainly be not less than 1,200 *pounds per acre, against* 500 *pounds* average for the State under old methods. This gives a gain of 700 pounds of seed cotton per acre, worth $25.00, or a total gain on the demonstration cotton plots alone of $157,500. Pursuing the same line, we may safely estimate that our demonstrations will each average thirty-five bushels of corn per acre against the ten-year average for the State of Alabama of only twelve bushels per acre old method. This gives a gain of twenty-three bushels per acre, worth at present prices $20.00. Hence we find on our 3,500 acres that we have a total increase in the corn crop

[1]MS Copy of report sent to Mr. Bradford Knapp, Washington, D. C., November 16, 1911.

valued at $70,000; $157,500 plus $70,000, gives a total of $227,500 per annum from demonstration plots alone. Add to this an equal increase secured by our cooperators and we have a total increase in crop of $455,000. Our results are a justification for the existence of the demonstration work. We have spent in this State this year, from all sources, about $60,000, and have received in return therefor not less than $455,000, or 750 per cent per annum on the investment."

Negro Farmers Eager for Help.

It is my observation that negro farmers are more eager for help and more amenable to instructions than the average white farmer.

My question of the farm demonstrators as to ability of these farmers to follow instructions reveals the fact that all agree the farmers are capable. The State of Florida reports 600 negro farmers following demonstration methods. One county in Alabama reports 500 listed as demonstrators, Oklahoma reports 77 demonstrators and 249 cooperators. J. B. Pierce, State Agent for farm demonstration work among Negroes in Virginia, writes that he has six local agents working under him with 1,000 negro farmers doing demonstration work. J. E. Blanton, of St. Helena Island, writes he has seventy negro farmers demonstrating with him, and so the story goes. Every agent who has tried it, and to whom I have talked, says the negro farmer is eager and willing to follow instructions, and usually fully competent to do so. We need more agents for Negroes, *and more white men willing to help the Negro in the absence of negro agents.*

Remarkable Results of the Work.

I went with Mr. Pierce, in Nottaway County, Virginia, to visit the home of Wm. Keaton, a Negro, who owns seventy acres for which he paid $900 several years ago. For years he had been living in a two-room house because he was making very little on his farm. He told me he was forced to work out at least half the year to get enough ready money to keep something for his family to eat. He had been making eight to ten bushels of corn per acre prior to his demonstration work. He began work on scientific lines four years ago, and is now raising forty bushels of corn to the acre on the same land that formerly produced only eight. He has built him a good two-story house of four rooms in front of the old one, and it is nicely furnished and was clean and neat. The yard fences were all white-washed, the house painted, flowers in the yard and rockers on the front porch. He has three good horses, three good milk cows, seven head of Berkshire hogs, a wagon, a buggy, and his whole farm has an air of prosperity. His face fairly beamed as he told me *farm demonstration had been his salvation.*

Or take another illustration: Jasper P. Lee, of Ware Neck, Gloucester County, Virginia. He owns only five acres in all. He was born a slave, but has acquired enough training to do the farm demonstration work. He raises forty bushels of corn to the acre instead of twenty, as on the old method. He has two horses, a good cow, a six-room house, which was well kept, and in it I was pleased to find a very good copy of Raphael's Madonna framed and hanging on the wall. This reminds me that in another negro farm home in Virginia I found not a bad reproduction of Sir Joshua Reynolds-West Window in New College. The woman in whose house I found this was a resident of Gloucester County also, and while she prized the picture highly, did not know just what it was.

Or to take one more simple illustration out of many dozens one could give. Mr. J. E. Blanton, the demonstration agent on St. Helena Island, kindly drove me all over the island to see the home and farm conditions. We stopped one day at the home of two brothers who now own and occupy jointly one of the old overseer houses of slavery days. These brothers were reared together, have always farmed side by side, and so each man had about an equal chance. Brother No. 1 agreed to tend part of his land on demonstration methods; No. 2 refused, saying he could farm as well as any agent and did not need help. They planted their corn side by side, there being simply a fence between. Each worked hard, for there was a degree of rivalry there. No. 1 made forty-two bushels per acre and No. 2 made nineteen. It goes without saying both will work on demonstration methods this coming year. One of the negro preachers told me rather shamefacedly that he had laughed at the idea of scientific farming, but he had made last year fifty-eight bushels to the acre. When asked what he had been making on the old method he did not want to tell, but when pressed said he had made twenty bushels on four acres. To the Negroes this new method of farming is nothing less than a blessing from heaven. It opens the door of hope to them. It makes it possible for them to see a time when they can have a respectable living and a decent home. The uplift of the negro race must be accomplished by means of the fulcrum of a sound economic progress, and here lies the hope of many a discouraged farmer. *What is needed is a demonstration agent in every county in the South to help these men out of their ignorance and despair into larger ideals and a larger hope.* Seeing what this work can do, the bankers and merchants in some places are paying the salary of such a demonstrator, believing it will more than repay them in added prosperity for the community.

Prosperity in Other Phases of Life.

But economic prosperity does not go alone. Wherever the farmers are doing better work it at once shows in the homes. As I remarked before I drove three days through Gloucester County, Virginia, and in all that time I did not see a single one-room cabin occupied. Most of the people have built four, five and six-room houses. I went into many of these homes and found them neat, clean and attractive. Also the churches take on at once a new appearance. I visited four in Gloucester County and found not a single window glass broken, the aisles carpeted, good lights and much more attractive houses than many a white church in which I have spoken. The schools, likewise, take on a new power where the people are prosperous. The people are able to pay better salaries, they get better teachers, and the children attend more regularly. Almost every demonstration agent writing me explicitly says the schools have improved since the demonstration work began. One agent writes: "We are just now trying to work out something in the line of amusements." Others tell how they interest the boys in corn clubs, of which I have not had time to speak. Still others tell of its influence in the home in the way of gardening clubs for girls. Speaking of its general influence on the life of the community, S. H. Murphy, a negro demonstration agent for Kenshaw County, South Carolina, writes: "It is a remarkable fact that the increased yields of corn and cotton have surprised some farmers to a certain degree, but what interests them most is the fact that they see the beginning of the possibilities of the soil, the "door of hope." Many who simply could not make a crop of corn are delighted. Incidentally, "King (?) Cotton's" throne is tottering for more reasons than low prices of that product. They see the possibilities in hogs and cattle with food for them. In February we called a farmers' conference, and in October re-enforced this with a county fair. Since the showing of hogs here five farmers have secured high-priced, pure-bred Berkshire sires. Of course these will help others, and will prove themselves among the best citizens of their communities (I mean the hogs)."

It has been estimated by workers in the Census Bureau that in 1910 Negroes were cultivating, either as owners, tenants or hired laborers, one hundred million acres of land. If farm demonstration work can double the yield of these millions of acres, the white people of the South will be stupid indeed if they do not insist that these negro farmers be given a full chance. Here is the opportunity for the white farm demonstrator to prove that he is a democrat indeed, and believes in an equal chance for all by helping his negro neighbor.

Spiritualization of Progress.

All this material prosperity must be spiritualized and idealized. I mean we must not allow these people simply to make money for the sake of making it. We must do for them just what must be done for all advancing people, we must set ideals before them which are worthy and Christian. Of this need for idealism in the country, President Butterfield well says:

"One grave danger to permanent progress is the low *level of ideals,* determined by community standards. It is not that the average ideals are lower than in the city. I think they are higher. But *they come perilously close to a dead level in immense areas of the country. . . . As a consequence the rural community is in constant danger of stagnation*—of settling down into the easy chairs of satisfaction. Rural life needs constant stimulus of imported ideas—a stimulus of suggestion apart from its daily routine.

"Moreover, rural ideals sometimes lack breadth and variety. Life in the country easily becomes monotonous, humdrum. It needs broadening as well as elevating. It needs variety, gaiety, but these changes can find their proper stimulus only in motives that are high and worthy. Hence an appeal must be made for the cultivation of ideals of personal development and neighborhood advancement.

"*Lack of ideals is in a sense responsible for the drift away from the farm.* Some people leave the country because they cannot realize their ideals in the existing rural atmosphere. Others go because they have no thought of the possibilities of country life. . . . Attention has been called to the fact that rural life is more full of poetry than any other. *But rural romance is often stifled in the atmosphere of drudgery and isolation.* This high sentiment is of the soul and can come only as the soul expands. It is not merely an enjoyment of trees, crops and animals. *It is in part a sense of exaltation born of contact with God at work.* It has in it an element of triumph because great powers are being harnessed for man's bidding. It has in it somewhat of the air of freedom because of dealing with forces free and wild except as they are held in leash by an unseen Master driver. It has in it much of worship, because of all the deep mysteries of seed and soil, and because of the everlasting, patient procession of the seasons and their vicissitudes. *I can conceive of preaching that would give to farm men and women a new birth of aspiration and hope, simply because it should set vibrating the chords of poetry and romance that are strung upon the harps* of men at work in God's out-of-doors, strings too often untouched by any hand save that of chance."

When the farm life of the Negro shall have been so far developed as to lay a deep, broad, economic foundation for his progress, when this economic welfare has found an expression in better schools and better churches, and when all the rural processes shall have been spiritualized, then shall we be beginning to solve the race question. Every white and colored man should be a well-wisher and willing worker to this end.

CHAPTER V

IMPROVEMENT IN RURAL SCHOOLS

STICKIN' TO DE HOE

I ain't got no edikashun
  But dis I kno' am true,
Dat raisin' gals too good to wuck
  Ain't nebber gwine to do;
Dese boys dat look good 'nuf to eat,
  But too good to saw de logs,
Am kay'n us ez fas' ez smoke,
  To lan' us at de dogs.

I s'pose dat I'm ol' fashun',
  But God made man to plow,
An' git his libbin by de sweat
  Dat trickles down his brow.
While larnin' an' all dem things
  Am mighty good fur sho',
De bes' way we kin make our pints
  Is stickin' to de hoe.

To fill de hed wid larnin'
  Dat de fingers kan't express,
To dis poor ig'nunt brudder
  Don't seem to be de bes';
To git de edikashun
  An' larn to work ez well,
Seems to my 'umble judgment,
  De thing dat's gwine to tell.
              —*Daniel Webster Davis*

CHAPTER V

IMPROVEMENT IN RURAL SCHOOLS

The overwhelming per cent of the negro people live in rural communities, so that whatever progress is to be made must come through better rural conditions. The rural school, therefore, has a unique opportunity to minister to the needs of the negro race; hence, it is a matter of paramount importance that these schools shall be thorough, progressive, and closely related to the needs of the community.

The importance of this agency is all the more clearly understood when we come to see the intense eagerness of the rural Negro for training. In the country where the excitement of the city has not distracted and spoiled the negro child, the majority of them can be found in school, and that quite regularly when school is in session. Thus in Kentucky, while only 51 per cent of the negro children of school age in the towns and cities during the years 1910-1911 enrolled in school, 66 per cent of the children of school age in rural communities were enrolled. On a visit to St. Helena Island, South Carolina, I found that there were scores of children eager to come to the school and walk from three to eight miles each way. One morning just after chapel service I found three boys just arriving. They were a little late, for which they looked a bit shamefaced, but I could never have the hardihood to call them tardy, for the teacher told me they lived ten miles away, which distance they walked twice each day regularly. Where a whole people are as eager as this, that institution which ministers to their hunger has an opportunity unbounded.

Weakness of the Present System.

It seems almost presumptious for one not actively engaged in public school work to attempt to criticise the present system. Yet, I do not do this without careful forethought. I have visited a great many rural negro schools in a number of States, have talked again and again with the men who are giving their lives to this field of school supervision, have read diligently the reports of all the State supervisors in the South, and have taken special care that the facts laid down here are carefully sifted. Rural schools of all types are poor enough, but the rural negro schools are bad beyond comprehension.

Buildings Inadequate.

The proverbial log cabin as a school-house is still not a thing of the past in the South. Florida had in 1910, 313 still in use. Of these, Negroes have just about their proportion as compared with the number used by the whites. But it does not help matters to say that some whites go to school in the same type of buildings. South Carolina has 1,777 school buildings for Negroes, costing on the average $246.88 for buildings and grounds. When we remember that this includes all the buildings and grounds in cities, we will readily see that the average country school building is a mere hut. This is certainly in keeping with my personal observations in this State. Of these buildings Prof. W. K. Tate, State Supervisor of Rural Schools, says: "The negro school-houses are miserable beyond all description. They are usually without comfort, equipment, proper lighting or sanitation." [1] Again he says in his report to the State Superintendent: "The negro school buildings are in most cases a serious reflection on our civilization. They are without adaptation to school work, are destitute of all proper

---

[1] "Forty-third Annual Report State Superintendent of Education of S. C.," p. 115.

furniture and equipment, frequently without window sash, usually unceiled, often without any kind of heating arrangements, and comfortless and unsanitary in the extreme. They are usually erected by private effort and without any sort of suggestion or direction from any competent authority."[1]

In Virginia the last biennial report gives for 1909, 544 log school-houses still in service, of which the Negroes use their full share. I visited one such school-house in Virginia, in which one of the trustees told me that in a room twenty feet square, with one small window, one teacher had had the year before ninety pupils enrolled, with an average daily attendance of sixty-six, and there were not any upper berths, either. How the teacher got them all in I could not possibly understand.

Texas, with her seventy million-dollar school fund, owns only 1,457 school-houses for Negroes, only 185 of which the Superintendent is willing to report as in good condition, 471 are in bad condition, and all the others only fair. Six hundred and eighty-two other negro schools are taught in rented buildings. I visited a large plantation on the Brazos River in Texas where between one and two hundred negro families are employed, and where it was reported the landlord cleared $40,000 in cash last year off his cotton crop, and yet the negro school-house was a bare shell, all dilapidated, and costing originally not more than two or three hundred dollars. There is not a State in the South that has anything like adequate buildings for its negro students. Every Southern white man who reads these lines ought to hang his head with shame that we have boasted of what we are doing for the Negro, and are still trying to give them training in places, many of which would not be good enough for a horse or a mule.

---

[2]"Forty-second Annual Report State Superintendent of Education of S. C.," p. 92.

Poor Sanitation.

One of the weakest places of the rural school is in its lack of sanitation. In most cases the sanitation cannot even be called poor; there is none. The superintendent of schools for Virginia reports for 1909 3,952 schools having outhouses, not all of them really sanitary, *and 3,051 schools with no toilet facilities whatever.* Inasmuch as this includes both city and country schools, and for both races, it will readily be seen that the rural negro schools would likely have not more than one school in five supplied with toilets. I have visited a great many country schools for Negroes in this and other States which would be listed as having toilets, but where there was only one toilet for both boys and girls. So this is not only a health question but a moral question. There can be no real morality fostered under conditions like these. Now, if our public schools are forced to become breeders of indecency and immorality, they surely cannot serve the purpose for which they were established— the making of efficient citizens.

Hookworm.

One outcome of this lack of proper sanitation is soil pollution, through which thousands of children, both white and black, become infected with hookworm. This pest is supremely a disease of the Negro, though it is fast becoming the plague of white people in the South. It is supposed that it was brought originally into this country by the slaves coming over from Africa, where it is exceedingly prevalent. This worm fastens itself to the interior of the intestines, where it sucks the blood of the person, thus making him aenemic, weak, listless, thick-headed, lazy. The worm does not multiply in the intestine, but the female lays thousands of eggs which pass out of the intestines, and if there are no toilets, these eggs are deposited on the ground, where, under favorable conditions of moisture, they hatch and live for as long as five or six months.

How the Hook Worm Enters the Body.

In the morning when there is dew the worm is very active, and as the barefoot boy or girl walks along, it fastens itself on the bare feet and begins burrowing in This makes the feet a little sore and we call it "toe itch," "ground itch," "dew poison," "cow itch," etc. These are just the terms of the common people to designate what the scientist knows to be hookworm. Of course they may also be swallowed with polluted water, or with raw vegetables that have not been properly cleaned. When once the hookworm enters the body it lives the life of a parasite, literally eating the blood of the person in whom it dwells. This one disease alone will explain thousands of cases of unambitious and lifeless boys and girls of both colors in the rural districts. For the sake of scientific accuracy, I quote in full a statement from the "Report of the Rockefeller Sanitary Commission, 1911":

"During the past year I have gathered statistics as to the privy conditions surrounding 4,825 American farm homes, located in six different States, and I find that 2,664, or about 55 per cent of them, have no privy of any kind. Of 2,499 homes tabulated as occupied by whites, 35.2 per cent have no privy, and of 2,326 houses tabulated as occupied by negroes, 76.8 per cent have no privy.

"These shocking sanitary conditions under which so many American rural families are living necessarily increase the causes of sickness and death, especially among the women and children, and they decrease the efficiency and laboring capacity among the men.

"The fact that the sanitary conditions surrounding the Negroes are so much worse than those surrounding the whites calls for very serious consideration, for it involves not only the health, efficiency and progress of the Negroes themselves, but of the whites also. So long as the Negro continues to live as he is living at present in the rural districts, his home will remain a reservoir from which all disease may spread to the whites, and the white man owes it to his own race that he lend a helping hand to improve sanitary surroundings of the Negro. One way this can be done is by obtaining support for instruction in hygiene in negro schools. Another way is by teaching the white landlords the rudiments of hygiene."[1]

Prevalence of the Disease.

I have talked with a number of State experts and have before me the reports of the Surgeon-General of the United States, and the various reports of the Rockefeller Sanitary Commission. The concensus of opinion of all these is that an alarmingly large per cent of the population in the South is infected. Dr. Stiles, of the United States Marine Hospital Service, in his report on hookworm infection in 1910, writes as follows:

"My present estimate is that not less than 30 per cent of the rural inhabitants of our Southern States have hookworm infection. In some restricted localities fully 90 per cent have the infection.

"Colleges are known in which over 30 per cent of the students show infection on microscopic examination. County schools are known in which 35 to 95 per cent of the pupils harbor hookworms. In view of the effect which hookworms have on the nervous system, including inhibiting effect on mental processes, this disease must be viewed as important in connection with the subject of education, more especially in the rural districts."[2]

---

[1] "Rockefeller's Sanitary Commission," p. 19.
[2] "Public Health Bulletin" No. 32, Washington, 1910.

Not A Matter of Indifference.

This horrible and widespread disease is not a matter of indifference to any Southern white man who believes in his country. It incapacitates the laboring classes for wealth-producing, thus making our section drop further and further behind in the economic race of America. It makes many thousands listless and indifferent, so that they drift into pauperism and then into crime. We must pay the bills not only of the law courts, jails, increased police force, etc., but we must pay the penalty of insecurity of property and life because of this criminal class. Lastly, these diseased persons become centers of contagion, scattering this deadly enemy wherever they go. The white men of the South have it within their power to see that this disease is eradicated. We have control of all the public schools. We can see that every school, both white and colored, has sanitary outhouses. We can see that every school has some simple instruction given in sanitation and hygiene; we can create sentiment by taking a personal interest in these problems, whether we are teachers, preachers or business men. In this work the Rockefeller Sanitary Commission, with its State agents and its host of district agents, is making such thorough investigation and doing such splendid work that it cannot fail to elicit the cooperation and hearty support of all who understand the need. The obligation is upon us, and in this tremendous task the small but increasing group of Negroes who are awake to this evil will be our surest guides and our able helpers.

Insufficient Playgrounds.

I wish to refer to this point again in the chapter on Association Work, but in mentioning the weak places of our public schools, one cannot pass over so glaring a fault as the fact of insufficient playgrounds and often no playgrounds whatever. Recently I visited a rural negro school in Virginia where a group of boys were attempting to play ball at recess. It was simply impossible to have a game, because the school only owned half an acre of land, and all around were trees, stumps and other obstructions. A ball could not be batted or thrown fifty feet without striking one of these obstructions. Of course the school could not be attractive to these boys, and as a result most of them will drop out at an early age. Of all the public schools of Virginia, 1,667 of them own half an acre or less, 1,332 own more than half an acre but less than an acre, and only the smallest proportion own sufficient land to give decent playgrounds. *No school should be built on less than a five-acre plot in the country, or less than three acres in the city.* This alone would do more to keep the children satisfied with the school than would any other one thing outside the personality and ability of the teacher.

Length of Term and Salaries.

The average salary paid all public school teachers in South Carolina during the term 1910-11, was for negro men $132.73, negro women $98.38. The length of term for towns was twenty-two weeks, that for the rural community thirteen weeks, or sixty-five days. It will therefore be readily seen that the rural teacher would not get anything like the above amount. This will further be seen when it is remembered that the average expenditure per enrollment is for white children $12.62, but is only $1.71 per negro child, or 13 cents per week, 52 cents per month. In a school of fifty pupils, which would be a large enrollment, there would be available for teachers' salary and all expenses of the school, $26.00 per month. The average school would be much below this.

In Florida the average length of a term is ninety-six days as compared with 110 days for the whites, and the average salary is $33.68 for men and $30.18 for women, per month. Here again the figures for the whole State are very much higher than for the rural districts. In Texas the average length of term in rural schools, both white and black, was 114½ days. If there is as great a disparity between white and colored in the country and those in the city, as elsewhere, it would reduce the rural colored schools to less than one hundred days. The average annual salary in these colored schools is for males $330.35, for females $264.24, or $53.29 and $42.47 per month, respectively. For the rural teachers this would, of course, be greatly reduced. Texas seems to be the only State in the South which gives anything like adequate remuneration to secure good negro teachers. The following table shows the facts of length of school terms for Negroes in a number of States, the percentage of enrollment, percentage daily attendance of those enrolled, and average salary of teachers.

According to this table in the States listed, 124 days is the longest average term for Negroes.

Teachers Poorly Prepared.

According to the report of the Superintendent of Education for the State of Texás, where the public school system is perhaps as good as can be found in the South, out of 13,116 rural teachers, 10,564 have had no college, normal or even high school education. This large number is trying to teach, when they themselves have not finished more than the seventh or eighth grade. It is a well-known fact that this is far above the preparation for the rural negro teachers. Of the 4,413 negro teachers holding first, second, third grade or permanent certificates, 3,427 held the two lowest rank certificates, that is third and second—equal to about fifth and sixth grade work in a good public school.

In Alabama for the year 1911, of the 2,384 negro teachers, 2,210, or 92 per cent, held either second or third grade

STATISTICS OF NEGRO PUBLIC SCHOOLS, ETC.
Latest Available Reports Used.

STATE	Length of School Term		Average Annual Salary of Teachers—Col.		Percentage of School Population Enrolled in School		Percentage Daily Attendance of Those Enrolled	
	White	Col.	Male	Female	White	Col.	White	Col.
Florida____	110	96	$161.66	$144.86	.65	.51	.61	.66
S. Carolina		65	132.73	98.38			.61	.66
Alabama__	127	95	169.00	150.00	.78	.49	.64	.65
Virginia___	130	122	Rural 162.78 186.78	27.27 167.89	.75	.50	.66	.61
Tennessee_	Not sep. as to color Rural____109 All_____120		Not separated as to sex or race Rural _____202.30 All_____237.42		.67	.54	.64	.65
Texas_____	132	124	330.35	264.24	.63	.61	.62	.58
North Carolina __	104.6	93.7	Not separated as to sex Rural_____95.91 All_____118.33		72.4	Rural 71.4 67.7	65.5	59.5

certificates. It is unnecessary to give further statistics. It is clearly a case of wretched "unpreparedness," and we need not wonder that the negro child does not make more rapid advancement.

Poor Supervision.

The last weakness which I shall mention—but by no means the last one that can be mentioned—is lack of proper supervision. In setting forth the need of better supervision I cannot do better than let Prof. W. K. Tate speak in the words of his last annual report:

"I wish once more to emphasize the value of proper supervision in the training of teachers. The City Superintendent usually finds a new recruit in his school awkward and inefficient. He must continually assist her in the management of her class and in the improvement of her methods. She progresses rapidly under the right kind of supervision. *The country teacher has almost none of this assistance.* The sole supervising officer is the County Superintendent, employed at a salary which assumes that he is to devote only a portion of his time to this work and responsible for a territory which makes it impossible for him to visit the schools more than once a year. There are counties in South Carolina in which the salary of the County Superintendent, with 300 teachers in his charge, is less than one-half the salary of the City Superintendent in the county seat with one-tenth the number of teachers. . . . During the year I have visited many schools in which three hours of demonstration work and practical suggestions would double the efficiency of an earnest but inexperienced teacher. . . . The education of the Negro in South Carolina is in the hands of the white race. The white trustees apportion the funds, select the teachers, and receive reports. The County Superintendent has the supervision of these schools in his hands. *We have expended this year $348,834.60 in the support of negro schools. I never visit one of these schools without feeling that we are wasting a large part of this money and are neglecting a great opportunity.*" [1] *.. There are literally scores of white County Superintendents who never visit a negro school, and often do not know where these schools are located.* This work cannot be made efficient by correspondence. If the white teachers need help, direction, encouragement, how much more do the negro teachers need this, and yet the colored teacher gets less than

---

[1] "South Carolina Report, 1911," pp. 105, 106, 115.

one-fourth the attention that the rural white teacher gets. This is poor economy, to put it mildly. If we spend from a quarter to a half million dollars in each Southern State annually on negro education, we ought at least to have business sagacity enough to see that it is well spent. The one way to bring this about is for the County Superintendents to give more careful supervision to these schools, and for the white boards of trustees to take more care in selecting teachers.

Summary of Weaknesses.

This statement of weaknesses seems almost too sweeping. And yet we have said nothing about the lamentable weakness of the curriculum, which is almost always a misfit. It has nothing that stirs the pride of the race in itself. All the books are written with white illustrations. Neither is there anything that connects the student with his environment. I visited a negro school some time since where the boys and girls in a third reader class were reading some fairy story so absolutely foreign to their conceptions that every child was calling the words mechanically without the barest conception of what the sentences meant. Why should not these text-books do what is most fundamental at present, help the race to understand its surroundings, the plants, the birds, the flowers, the crops, the people? Why should they not give us some simple stories of the lives of the best of the race, thus helping to build a race pride? Why not acquaint the children with the simple, beautiful poems of Dunbar, one of the best writers of the race? There is a great need for the careful planning of a new course of study for these schools.

Neither have I spoken of the barrenness and lack of attractiveness of the school grounds and buildings. In my judgment one of the chief ways of keeping more of these boys and girls in the country is to give them more attractive schools, churches and homes. No wonder the Negro is leaving the country. There is nothing there to attract him. If we would spend less time berating him for moving to town, and more time giving him an efficient and attractive rural school, we would show a larger statesmanship.

If we could secure more comfortable buildings, establish more sanitary practices, give longer terms, better teachers, more thorough supervision and have courses more adapted to the needs of the race, we would be beginning at least to meet the needs of the situation.

More Hopeful Features.

However, there are many signs of real progress. Perhaps the first is the movement toward the consolidation of some of the smaller, more inefficient schools into larger ones, where better buildings, better playgrounds, two or more teachers and better grading can be had. In Gloucester County, Virginia, I recently visited a school where four small struggling schools had been consolidated. The colored people of the four communities got together, raised $400 in cash to help buy the site and a good dwelling, and then asked the board to give the remaining $600 necessary. No sooner was this done than the people themselves began work to raise half of $1,500 to build a new three-room building. At the time of my visit the necessary cash was collected and in the bank. Instead, therefore, of four shabby school buildings, each located on a little cramped half-acre lot, and taught by a poorly prepared and inexperienced woman, they are to have a first-class, comfortable and attractive three-room building, with six acres of land for playgrounds, three better trained and more experienced teachers, 150 pupils instead of thirty or forty each, which will at once add new zest to the whole school life. This is real progress and this movement is rapidly spreading. It is estimated by the Southern Education Association that 1,166 schools employing an equal number of teachers, have been abandoned in the last half decade in the South. In these schools 28,204 children were taught. All of these schools have been consolidated with other schools and all children are now getting much better instruction. Not the least benefit of consolidation comes from the larger associations into which the child enters in the larger school. One of the banes of country life is isolation, and consolidated schools help to remove this evil. Isolation is particularly the difficult problem with negro rural schools. The older boys and girls drop out early to go to work, so the small handful of children in a little rural school, without leadership, become about the most abandoned, forlorn-looking groups one can possibly find. This of necessity deters children from staying in school. The consolidated school brings together the few older students from the various communities and welds them into a group of leaders, thus making school much more attractive. More attractive schools is one of the largest factors in making the Negro population satisfied.

Negro Self-Help.

One of the elements in this movement for consolidation is the fact of the negro's willingness to bear a goodly part of the financial burden. The Superintedent of Education of North Carolina says:

"In justice to the negro and for the information of some of our people who have been misled into thinking that too large a part of the taxes that the white people pay is spent for the education of the negro, it may be well in the outset to give a brief statement of the facts in regard to the apportionment of the school fund. As it is well known, under Section 4116 of the School Law, the apportionment of the school fund in each county is practically placed absolutely under the control of the County Board of Education, the only restriction laid upon the board therein being that the funds shall be apportioned among the schools of each township in such a way as to give equal length of term as nearly as possible, having due regard to the grade of work to be done, the qualifications of teachers, etc. The Constitution directs that in the distribution of the fund no discrimination shall be made in favor of either race. This report shows that in 1910 the negroes of city and rural districts received for teachers' salaries and building schoolhouses $373,390.55 for 238,091 children of school age. The whites received for the same purpose $1,924,704 for 497,077 children of school age. The negroes, therefore, constitute about 32 per cent of the school population and receive in the apportionment for the same purposes less than 17 per cent of the school money. This report shows that the negroes paid for schools in taxes on their own property and polls about $163,417.89, or nearly one-half of all that they received for school purposes."[1]

Some have supposed that the Negro is paying as much direct school taxes as he is getting returned in school funds. This can hardly be maintained. Mr. Coon, of Wilson, N. C., attempted to prove that the Negroes in the South pay more school taxes than are spent on their schools. Thus in Virginia he claimed the Negroes paid $507,305 in school taxes, but had only $489,228 spent on their schools. But the figures were based on proportions of Negroes to whites and had glaring errors. State Superintendent Eggleston is a real friend of the negro race, and an advocate of good negro schools, yet in a letter to the United States Commissioner of Education, dated October, 1909, and printed in the Virginia Journal of Education, he makes clear that Mr. Coon's figures for school taxation are about five times too large, and the Negroes paid directly less than one hundred thousand toward the school fund, while nearly five hundred thousand was spent. While the Negro does not pay a large

[1]"North Carolina Report, 1909-10," pp. 54, 55.

direct tax, every student of political economy knows full well that the laboring man ultimately pays most of the taxes. He it is who creates the wealth, and in the last analysis therefore the negro laborer pays his full share of the taxes.

The important item in Virginia, however, *is that they do pay nearly one hundred thousand* direct school tax. It seems perfectly marvelous that a race starting with nothing could accumulate sufficient property in one State to pay one hundred thousand in school taxes, and nearly three times that much more for taxes for other purposes. But it is sheer nonsense to claim that any part of the community shall have only that which it pays. *The purpose of public education is to help those who cannot pay. The State has absolutely no business in educational work save to make better citizens of all, and surely it cannot afford to neglect those who most sorely need help.* Fortunately, however, the Negro is paying an increasing proportion of his school bill through taxes.

Besides paying an increasing amount of school taxes, they are also doing valiantly by way of personal and voluntary contributions. There are many of the rural schools in the South where the Negroes have raised the money and replaced old buildings with new and comfortable ones. In many other cases they have raised fully half the amount needed to erect a building before asking the school board for an appropriation. This is a most hopeful sign.

The New Type of Curriculum.

In many of the rural schools there is a new type of work done. The study is much more directly related to the community needs. The boys, along with their reading, writing and arithmetic, are taught how to make shuck mats, how to do simple school gardening, and the girls are taught sewing, cooking and the simple principles of good housekeeping.

This kind of study immediately reacts on the practical

ideals of the students. A number of schools I visited had raised the money to build fences around the school yards, the yards were clean and well kept, shrubbery had been set out, the house itself had been whitewashed or painted and everything had an air of prosperity.

One school in Henrico County, Virginia, had raised money and put in sanitary toilets, laid cement walks, set privet bushes and fenced the yard. Another had fenced the yard, bought a private drinking cup for each child, thus teaching a good lesson in hygiene, and had bought a range and all necessary utensils for cooking.

Another consolidated school with three teachers, taught in a building with four rooms, had raised enough money to fit up the fourth room as a kitchen with ample cupboards, bins, tables and range. They had also bought and made neat white curtains for all the windows, as had also been done by a number of the other schools.

Still another school had raised enough money to build an addition to the old building, put in better furniture and fenced the yard.

Effect on the Community.

All of this has a most marked effect on the whole community. Every child learns to be more neat, clean and self-respecting. He learns some of the simple laws of hygiene and sanitation. He begins to take a pride in doing some commonplace things. He learns that work is dignified and that education is not to help one to escape work, but to fit one to do work better. All of this is uplifting to the homes from which the children come.

But besides this, the boys take home some of the mats and baskets they have made, and the girls take home some of their aprons, simple table covers, etc. These little things add much to the attractiveness of the very barren rural home. They immediately give a new pride in the home, make home

seem more worth while, make love for home grow and consequently affect moral standards.   One cannot measure the
real moral effect of any single piece of work well and
faithfully done, and that is what this new type of school
is attempting to teach.   The three R's are not taught less,
but much better and more effectively because of this practical side.

In the Homes.

In visiting the rural homes where children have had this
kind of training, I have almost always found the house
cleaner, the people happier and better satisfied.   One notes
again and again the pride of the parents when a visitor
remarks on a neat scarf, or a good door mat, or a useful
basket seen in the home, and they are all too glad to tell you
that Mary or John did that at the school.

Supervision.

There are three distinct gains being made in this direction.   First, is that of a larger amount of time and attention
given by county and division superintendents to the rural
negro schools.   This brings the best type of white men in
touch with the teachers and those children who really have
ambition to better their conditions.   One of the largest contributions which the Southern white man can make to the
Negro's education is through visitation to the rural schools
by the County Superintendent.   Prof. W. K. Tate says:

"In South Carolina we simply turn over a certain portion of the school fund to the negro schools and expect the
most ignorant teachers of the State, without any suggestions or directions, to adapt to the special needs of the negro
schools a course of study and text-books designed primarily
for white children." [1]

It has been my privilege to visit a great many of the
rural schools in company with the division superintendents.

[1]"South Carolina Report, 1911," p. 116.

I spent a whole day last fall in the buggy of Mr. Arthur D. Wright, Division Superintendent of Henrico County, Virginia, visiting a number of his schools. The very fact that he was interested enough to do this work put new enthusiasm in the teachers in addition to the advice and counsel he was able to give. We must have an increasing number of our choicest Southern men who will consider this work a part of their duty and an opportunity for splendid service.

State Supervision.

In most of the Southern States in the past, the only attention the State Superintendent paid to negro schools was to get the enrollment in order to swell his report figures. It is to be hoped this is becoming a thing of the past. Virginia has led the way in securing the services of one of the choicest young educators, Mr. Jackson Davis, a Virginia gentleman of the best type, and a Phi Beta Kappa graduate of William and Mary College, who gives his entire time to supervising the rural negro schools of the State. He works through the Division Superintendents and the Industrial Supervisors, and visits enough schools himself to become a statesman in this phase of educational work. South Carolina has the funds in hand for the employment of a man for similar services. Kentucky has just secured the services of Mr. Button for this work. This is the most business-like and statesman-like move yet made for the upbuilding of the rural negro school.

Supervisors of Industrial Work.

Through the million-dollar gift of Miss Anna T. Jeans, under the supervision of Dr. James H. Dillard, of New Orleans, funds are available for the employment of 111 negro teachers annually. These teachers are known as Industrial Supervisors. One usually has supervision of all the industrial work carried on in the rural negro schools of a county or parish. This teacher visits each school in the county just as often as possible, spending half a day or a day in each. His or her work is to encourage and train the regular teacher in this industrial side of the school work and help in its inauguration, and at times of difficulty.

Henrico County, Virginia.

One of the best illustrations of this work is to be found in Henrico County, Virginia, the county in which Richmond is located. Conditions here are most favorable because Mr. Jackson Davis, now the State Supervisor of rural negro schools, was formerly Division Superintendent of Henrico County, and gave it its policy; second, because the present Division Superintendent, Mr. Arthur D. Wright, is a fine type of aggressive worker, much interested in this side of his duties; and third, because they have been extremely fortunate in getting a splendid Industrial Supervisor for the county in the person of Virginia Randolph, the best type of negro woman with training, of whom Prof. Wright says in his report, June, 1911: "No public servant has worked more faithfully or more conscientiously than Virginia Randolph, the pioneer in the work, and, I believe, without peer as to her devotion to duty and consecration of service or as to the practical results of her work." There are twenty-four rural negro schools in this county with an enrollment of 1,456 pupils and an average daily attendance of 77 per cent. It will be noted at once what a high average attendance this is. Far above that of any of the schools given in an earlier table. The first result of this industrial work, therefore, is to raise the daily attendance by one-fourth, *i. e.,* from 61 per cent, which is the average for the State of Virginia, to 77 per cent for Henrico County. The next important result of this type of training is that a far larger per cent of the school population is enrolled than formerly.

TABLE NO. 1.

1908 AND 1911—A COMPARISON

BROOKLAND.

	1908.	1911.	Gain.	Loss.
Negro school population............	638	674	36	
Whole number enrolled.............	404	447	43	
Per cent. school population enrolled..	63%	66%	3%	
Average monthly enrollment........	326	325		1
Average daily attendance...........	262	258		4
Per cent. in A. M. E. in A. D. A....	80%	80%		

FAIRFIELD.

	1908.	1911.	Gain.	Loss.
Negro school population............،	680	505		175
Whole number enrolled.............	267	308	41	
Per cent. school population enrolled..	39%	61%	22%	
Average monthly enrollment........	216	242	26	
Average daily attendance...........	189	209	20	
Per cent. A. M. E. in A. D. A.......	87%	87%		

TUCKAHOE.

	1908.	1911.	Gain.	Loss.
Negro school population............	583	481		102
Whole number enrolled.............	264	260		4
Per cent. school population enrolled..	45%	54%	9%	
Average monthly enrollment........	210	195		15
Average daily attendance...........	155	160	5	
Per cent. A. M. E. in A. D. A.......	74%	82%	8%	

VARINA.

	1908.	1911.	Gain.	Loss.
Negro school population............	496	431		65
Whole number enrolled.............	226	243	17	
Per cent. school population enrolled..	46%	56%	10%	
Average monthly enrollment........	185	172		13
Average daily attendance...........	130	128		2
Per cent. A. M. E. in A. D. A.......	70%	74%	4%	

EXPLANATORY NOTE.—The decrease in Negro school population in three districts is due to the fact that during this period a considerable portion of Henrico was annexed to the city of Richmond. A very large percentage of the school population of Brookland and Fairfield is suburban, and attends more regularly than the other two districts. It is significant to note that the two rural districts show material increases in the percentage of the average monthly enrollment in average daily attendance. It is also significant that each district shows a material increase in the percentage of the negro school population enrolled, Fairfield showing an increase from 39 per cent. to 61 per cent.

TABLE NO. 2.

THREE YEARS' WORK.

NOTE.—The following figures show the amounts raised each year since the beginning of this work by each school. All of this money, except a balance of about $400, now in the several treasuries, has been spent in providing materials for the industrial work and improving the grounds and buildings of the schools.

		—AMOUNT RAISED—		
		1908-9.	1909-10.	1910-11.
Brookland......	Barton Heights.....	*$ 50.05	$ 73.25	$ 100.81
	Broad St. Road....	10.00	10.02	82.66
	Carlton Street......	....	3.10	17.01
	Coal Pit..........	5.00	5.51	40.00
	Jeter	6.63	23.20	65.93
	Mountain Road....	23.00	38.42	110.00
	Pole Road.........	25.00	50.35	116.66
Fairfield........	Benedict	3.02	8.00	29.20
	Boar Swamp.......	3.00	14.35	57.50
	New Bridge........	8.38	6.10	21.11
	White Oak Swamp.	10.35	42.16	33.15
	Woodville	7.85	45.75	72.20
Tuckahoe.......	Carbon Hill........	14.18	32.00	71.00
	Greens	9.00	12.50	85.00
	Quioccasin	15.34	20.00	107.54
	Springfield	15.10	*75.00	36.49
	Westwood	12.00	15.00	*130.00
	Zion Town.........	29.47	25.00	33.45
Varina..........	Bethel	9.42	16.00	29.24
	Chatsworth	3.00	8.46	35.63
	Gravel Hill........	40.80	50.00	58.20
	St. James..........	10.00	15.00	25.20
	Sydney	5.30	6.62	26.00
Totals for county.............		$315.89	$595.79	$1,383.98

*Denotes the school each year raising the largest amount.

In a number of schools this increased per cent is as high as 20, as will be seen from the accompanying table No. 1, and in one case there was an increase of 41 per cent.

A third result of this industrial training is clearly seen in the amount of money the children themselves raise for school improvements, as is indicated in the table No. 2, taken from the 1911 report of the District Superintendent.

What the Industrial Work Is.

This industrial work requires six hours per week of every child and does not in any sense make it impossible to do thorough teaching along other lines. The following extracts from reports of individual teachers will indicate just what was undertaken and its results:

"Barton Heights School reports: Planted flowers, laid a walk around side of school, whitewashed fence, purchased two lamps, clock, tables, dishes, kitchen articles; taught cooking, sewing, carpentry, preserving, canning.

"Carlton Street School reports: Taught cabinet making from boxes, sewing, paper folding. Pictures donated by Dr. King of the Virginia Union University. A rented building.

Pole Road School reports: Taught cooking, sewing, woodwork and basketry. Bought flag, water coolers and individual drinking cups, shades, curtains, tools. Set out hedge and whitewashed trees and fences. Built woodhouse. Repaired outhouse.

"Benedict School reports: Taught sewing, raffia work, drawing, carpentry, whitewashed school, painted interior, patched doors and windows and bought set of carpenter's tools.

"White Oak Swamp School reports: Taught shoemaking, sewing, basketry, shuck mat making and carpentry. Put up fence, put new roof on school, built and whitewashed woodhouse and planted flowers.

"Quioccasin School reports: Taught sewing, shuck mat-making, basketry, cooking and woodwork. Painted building inside. Whitewashed outhouses, painted yard benches, sowed grass seed."[1]

Real Training.

This is real education. It not only dignifies labor by fitting the child to do something well and have a pride in it, but it directly affects the ideals of the community. It also makes the school the center of a larger life and thus contributes to the keeping of the boys in the county where they can find the largest life for themselves, and at the same time can be of the greatest force in the economic progress of the section. I could only wish that there might be ten times the money available that the Anna T. Jeans fund furnishes, so that an industrial supervisor might be placed in every county in the South. In this connection it should be said that a supervising teacher is never placed in a county without it is heartily requested by the County Superintendent. The teacher is selected by the County Superintendent, and to him reports are rendered. There are scores of counties now begging for such supervising teachers, but the money is not available to supply the demand. Here is the chance of a lifetime for some philanthropist to furnish such a fund. It would mark an epoch in Southern life.

Better Trained Teachers.

Lastly, attention must be called to the real progress being made in the training of teachers. Most of the output of the better negro schools is readily absorbed into the teaching profession. When China threw over her old educational system she suddenly realized she had no teachers, so she put her sons to school to all the world. This is the situation with the Negro. He has few teachers, but he can-

---

[1] "Third Annual Report, Henrico County, Va., Schools," p. 14.

not put his children to school where he pleases. He must wait until a sufficient number of teachers are trained to give his children instruction.

It is not at all strange, therefore, that the great majority of negro private schools are putting most emphasis on training teachers, neither is it strange that a very large per cent of the graduates of institutions like Hampton and Tuskegee, go into the school-room. These schools could render the South no greater service than that of sending out teachers who are not trained in head alone, but in hand and heart.

Every teacher who attempts to instruct negro children in the country needs to have careful training in agriculture and in the simple crafts. This immediately gives him or her a common interest with the community, and a hold upon the life of the pupils. At the Normal School for Negroes, Petersburg, Va., every girl has to take at least three years of instruction in agriculture, and two years in domestic science. The advantage of this is seen when one finds graduates from that school invariably holding places of real leadership in the community where they work. They have a sympathy for and a point of contact with the people among whom they labor. No man who visits the rural schools can for one moment begrudge the money spent in the various negro schools of the South for the training of capable, high-minded, true teachers.

The light slowly dawns over the far horizon. It has been long coming, but it is slowly driving back the clouds and darkness. More money spent on buildings and grounds, better sanitation, better supervision by white superintendents and colored industrial teachers, better trained teachers, and more sympathetic cooperation on the part of the Southern white man will hasten the day when our brothers in black shall know the truth, and the truth shall make them free.

CHAPTER VI

WHAT THE WHITE CHURCHES ARE NOW DOING FOR THE NEGRO

OL' MISTIS

Oh, de times is fas' a-changin',
   Ez de years ar' rollin' on,
An' de days seem mighty lonesum',
   Sense de good ol' times is gon'.
While I'm 'joycin' in my freedum,
   Nor wish fur slab'ry days,
Yit it warms my heart to 'member
   Sum good ol'-fashun ways.

Ub all de plezzun mem'riz,
   Dar's one dat fills my heart,
'Tis de thought ub dear ol' Mistis,
   An' 'twill nebber from me part.
No matter what de trubble
   De Lord wuz pleased to sen',
We had jes' to tell ol' Mistis,
   She would alwa's be a fren'.

Ef de oberseer 'buze us,
   An' frum de lash we'd run,
An' weary, col', an' starvin',
   Afread to kum back hom',
Jes' git word to ol' Mistis,
   She'd smoov de trubble o'er
An' back we'd kum a sneakin',
   An' hear ub it no mo'.

When sickness, kheer an' sorrow
   Gib nights ub akin' pain,
An' tears frum werry eyelids
   Kum pou'in down like rain;
Racked wid pains an' scotched wid febers,
   Wid lim's a-growin' col',
She had lin'ments fur de body,
   An' de Bible fur de soul.
               —Daniel Webster Davis.

CHAPTER VI

WHAT THE WHITE CHURCHES ARE NOW DOING FOR THE NEGRO

Many people have supposed that the early slaves came into possession of the Christian message by the mere accident of proximity to the white men who professed this religion. To such persons the one source of religious instruction for Negroes lay in the public service of the white churches, to which services the servants, particularly the house servants, were always admitted. It has not been generally known, even among the younger generation of Southern men, that there were any systematic plans for the propagation of the gospel among slaves outside this accidental method of sharing in the Sabbath services. Indeed, a well-trained colored man has said that he did not know there were ever many white missionaries to the Negroes before the war. But this plan of attendance at the white church would not have reached the great mass of Negroes on the plantation, where the white people were so few as frequently not to have any church at all. So if there was to be any gospel preached to the great mass of farm slaves it must be done through direct rather than accidental work.

Plantation Owners Not Indifferent.

As early as 1706, in the report of one of the missionaries sent out by the Society for the Propagation of the Gospel, we read, "Parents and masters were endued with much good will and a ready disposition to have their children and servants taught the Christian religion."[1] There

[1] Jones' "The Religious Instruction of Negroes in U. S."

was some indifference, but little opposition to missionary work among the slaves during the first century and half of slavery in America. Real opposition arose after a few insurrections of Negroes and also after some of the churches had taken a strong stand against slavery. In 1800 the Methodist Conference passed a very drastic resolution condemning slavery, and for many years following that time slave owners looked upon most preachers and missionaries as agitators who might easily do much to make the slaves dissatisfied with their condition.

In spite, however, of this fear of the missionaries, and perhaps partly that they might control the type of work done, two associations of planters were organized in Georgia in 1830 with the distinct purpose "of affording religious instruction to the Negroes by their own efforts, and by missionaries employed for the purpose. The first was formed by Rev. Joseph Clay Stiles in McIntosh County, embracing the neighborhood of Harris' Neck, which continued in operation for some time, until by the withdrawment of Mr. Stiles' labors from the neighborhood, and the loss of some of the inhabitants by death and removals, it ceased. The second was formed in Liberty County by the Midway Congregational Church and the Baptist Church under the respective pastors, and with one suspension from the absence of a missionary, has continued its operation to the present time" (1842).[1]

Instructions to Overseers About Religious Service.

The old manuscripts of instructions to overseers concerning the management of plantations, throw much light on the attitude of slave owners toward the religious instruction of Negroes. In a manuscript in the possession of Mr. Stovall, Stovall, Miss., J. W. Fowler writes to his overseer of a Mississippi bottom cotton plantation as follows:

---

[1] "Gospel Among the Slaves," Harrison & Barnes, p 75.

"I greatly desire that the gospel be preached to the Negroes when the services of a suitable person can be procured. This should be done on the Sabbath; day time is preferable, if convenient to the minister."[1]

Again he writes:

"I would that every human being have the gospel preached to them in its original purity and simplicity; it therefore devolves upon me to have these dependents properly instructed in all that pertains to the salvation of their souls; to this end whenever the services of a suitable person can be secured, have them instructed in these things—in view of the fanaticism of the age it behooves the master or overseer to be present on all such occasions. They should be instructed on Sundays in the day time if practicable; if not then, on Sunday night."[2]

As early as 1673 we find evidence that the leaders of the English church were solicitous about the religious life of the slaves in the colonies. During this year Mr. Baxter published his "Christian Directory," in which he has a chapter of "Directions to those Masters in Foreign Plantations who have Negroes and Other Slaves." In 1702 Rev. Samuel Thomas was sent by the Society for the Propagation of the Gospel, to become the first missionary to the Indians and Negroes in South Carolina. He died in 1706 and was succeeded by Dr. LeJean, who worked very successfully among the Negroes until 1717, when he died, and was succeeded by Mr. Ludlow. About this time a number of missions were established by this missionary society as widely separated as New York and the Carolinas.

In 1738 the Moravians established missions exclusively for the Negroes. A year previous to this Count Zienzendorf visited London, where he met General Ogelthorpe and the trustees of Georgia and plans were laid for the sending of

---

[1] "Documentary History of American Industrial Society," p. 114.
[2] Idem, p. 115.

missionaries to Georgia. The two missionaries did not, how-ever, reach Georgia, but made a tour through Virginia, Maryland, and North Carolina preaching the gospel to Negroes. They reported opposition on the part of masters, but in such terms as to indicate that the masters were them-selves doing something for the training of Negroes: "Va-rious proprietors," they reported, "however avowing their determination not to suffer strangers to instruct their Negroes, as they had their own ministers, whom they paid for that purpose, our brethren ceased from their efforts." [1]

Methodists' Missions.

Methodism was introduced into America in 1766, and the first missionaries sent out by Mr. Wesley in 1769. From this time on to the revolution, there were a number of re-vivals, particularly in Virginia and North Carolina, in which the Methodists and Episcopalians participated, and many Negroes heard the gospel. One letter states, "the chapel was full of white and black;" another, "hundreds of negroes were among them with tears streaming down their faces;" still another, "In general, the white people were within the chapel and the black people without." The first statistics as to colored members of the Methodist Church are given in 1786, when they number 1,890.

Episcopalians and Baptists.

Before the Revolution the Episcopalian Church was al-most the only religious influence in the State of Virginia, and consequently almost all of the religious instructions of Negroes in that State fell to their care. The Baptist Church was established in this country in 1639, but grew slowly in the South and West until the time of the Revolution, at which time there were Baptist congregations in most of the Southern States and an aggressive work for Negroes was

---

[1] Harrison & Barnes' "Gospel Among the Slaves," p. 48.

being carried on. They had ordained negro preachers as early as 1723, working, of course, under the supervision of the whites.

Presbyterians.

This group of Christians entered America about 1669 and held their first Presbytery in 1705. Themselves fugitives from tyranny, they opposed slavery from the first. As early as 1818 the Assembly fully set forth its conviction on this topic, beginning with the words, "We consider voluntary enslaving of one part of the human race by another as a gross violation of the most precious and sacred rights of human nature." They early began active work for the slaves.

Missionary Effort After the Revolution.

At the close of the Revolution all of the missionaries sent out from England by the Society for the Propagation of the Gospel, were withdrawn and all work was henceforth carried on by the native churches. There was no lack of enthusiasm. In 1806 the Baptist Church in South Carolina could report thirty-five hundred negro members, while by 1813 they reported forty thousand for the whole country. In 1816 the Presbyterians appointed Dr. Rice, of Virginia, as special missionary to the Negroes, and in 1833 drew up very strong resolutions urging a progressive work among the slaves. Scarcely a Bishop of the Episcopal Church failed to emphasize this work, and special helpers were appointed to give attention to the same. The following paragraph from a statement of Rev. Samuel S. Bishop will show the activity of this branch of the church:

"In 1859 there were recorded 468,000 members [colored] of the various churches in the South, of which it is perhaps fair to assume that more than 50,000 were baptized members of our church. There are now about 18,000 communicants in the whole church, 10 independent parishes and about 200 chapels and missions."[1]

The Methodists were very active, reporting twelve thousand two hundred and fifteen (12,215) members in 1797, and in 1860 they reported two hundred and seven thousand (207,000) members. Between 1829 and 1864 the Southern Conferences of Methodism gave $1,873,466.27, which supported missionaries set aside for negro evangelism, there being at one time (1860) three hundred and twenty-seven white Southern missionaries of this church giving their entire time to the work.

Method of Work.

A minister who labored in these fields describes the method of work as follows:

"The gospel was preached to the Negroes in common with the whites everywhere throughout the South, and in many places, smaller stations especially, a negro mission was attached to the work of the pastor, and once a month or oftener the pastor gave a part of the Sabbath to the 'colored charge.' In regular stations of the larger classes the afternoon was usually a special time allotted to the Negroes, and the only exception to this rule was in the large cities, where the Negroes were sufficiently numerous to form pastoral charges of their own. To those experienced and often able ministers were regularly appointed."[2]

Missionary Efforts Since 1860.

One of the very serious, if not the most serious result of the Civil War arose during the reconstruction period, when the Negro and Southern white man became estranged. This was disastrous in the extreme for all concerned. It was a dire calamity to the whole country because it left the

---

[1]"The Church Among the Negroes," Samuel H. Bishop.
[2]"Gospel Among the Slaves," Harrison-Barnes, p. 325.

laborers of our entire section without direction, control or encouragement. It was disastrous to the Southern white man because it made it impossible for him to save the Negro from blunders, and, through that, save himself untold suffering. It was doubly disastrous to the Negro, for it set him adrift without a friend who understood him, and at the same time robbed him of that splendid training he had been receiving from the white man for generations.

And yet this calamity could scarcely have been averted. The more I have studied this question the more I have come to realize how it all must have looked to the Northern man. To him it must have seemed a hopeless situation. He heard more of the one cruel master, and sworn enemy of freedom than he heard of nine other men who were as kindly as the system would allow them to be, and who would gladly have freed their slaves, as so many others had done, had the thing seemed at all practical. It was inevitable, therefore, that the Northern man should distrust the intentions of the South, and this distrust incapacitated him to see the fearful blunders of the reconstruction.

On the other hand, the Southern men returned from the war to find their property destroyed, their homes often burned, here and there a Negro who had grown arrogant and unbearably insolent, a foreign army administering their government, and their very own slaves set against them. It was inevitable that they should feel that the North was attempting to humiliate them in the extreme. What man would not have recoiled from the instrument used to crush his pride and destroy his leadership? That instrument was the Negro.

Meanwhile the poor Negro was hopelessly bewildered. He first expected forty acres and a mule, but had little idea of working either. Then he began to feel—for he was told it was true—that he was fully able to govern the land. He was not to blame for believing he could do what no human ever did—step out of illiterate slavery into full-fledged liberty, out of the corn fields into legislative halls.

When one looks at the whole picture with its colossal failures and mistakes, one wonders how it could ever have happened. There were honest men, many of them, in the North; there were heroic, true, genuine souls in vast numbers in the South; the Negro had proven himself capable of deep fidelity and true devotion during those dark days—and yet somehow there seemed to be just enough bad element from all sides to blind and befuddle all. In the awful tragedy of those years the white man lost his most devoted and trusted follower, and the black man lost his truest protector and friend.

If the old friendly relationship could have continued after the war—as it would have done largely, but for the horrors of reconstruction—the churches of the South, at the rate of progress they had made from 1844 to 1860, would have evangelized every Negro in the South long since. But this fatal split so embittered both sides that the white man did not care to work for the Negro, and the Negro did not care to have work done for him by his former master. In the chaos of the hour destruction reigned supreme.

Northern and Southern Churches.

It was natural, therefore, that the Northern churches should be the first ones in the field to preach the gospel to the liberated slaves. Many of the slaves continued for some time to attend the white churches of their former masters, but these churches dropped for a while all aggressive evangelizing of the freedmen. Gradually, as the air has cleared, and as men have gotten away from the passion of war, the Southern churches have taken up the work again. *The time is now ripe for every church in America to join hands in doing a great aggressive work for this belated people.* The Northern churches have the money and we of the South have the men. If we would only unite on a comprehensive and statesmanlike policy we might easily lift the Negro out of his present poverty, ignorance and sin into a growing knowledge of God, within the next two generations.

Lines of Work.

There are a number of distinct lines of effort carried on by the white churches for the Negro. These include assistance in the building of negro churches, evangelistic work through missionaries, both white and colored; Sunday school efforts, largely in the cities, where white teachers are available, and educational work of all grades. The Northern churches have put larger emphasis on church building and education; the Southern churches have put most emphasis on evangelism, Sunday school work, etc.

Church Buildings.

It is estimated that the negro churches in the South own $40,000,000 worth of property. This enormous sum of property has been accumulated from a variety of sources. First, the Negroes themselves have given a very large share, probably more than half of this. Second, the Southern white people as individuals have contributed a very large amount of money. This is particularly true of the smaller churches which serve the laboring classes. Every member in a congregation of this kind, when the house is being erected, takes with him a church card, with spaces for dimes, quarters and half dollars, and every time he meets a white friend or acquaintance he asks a contribution. It is a rare Southern man who will not respond to this call from his hired man or woman. Of course, no one can estimate just how much has been given in this way, but the amount would likely reach several millions.

The third source of funds for these churches, is from the organized missionary agencies of the Southern white churches. This does not represent a very considerable sum. The last source is that of the missionary agencies of Northern white churches. Thus the Board of Missions for Freedmen of the Presbyterian Church in the United States of America reports for the year ending May 11, 1911, a total expenditure in negro work of $145,489.48, of which $65,-109.01 was spent on church erection, church repairs, contingent expenses and ministerial support. The Episcopal Church, which is both a Northern and Southern church combined, is likewise aiding in the erection of simple chapels for the use of their negro communicants. This work is not very extensive, inasmuch as they only have eighteen thousand members among the Negroes of the country. The Congregational Church gives assistance to one hundred and fifty negro churches with an aggregate membership of about ten thousand. Unfortunately, the figures are not so tabulated as to indicate the exact amount spent on church buildings.

Missionary and Evangelistic Effort.

The Episcopal Church carries on its regular work among the Negroes through the direct channels of the church, the white bishops having direct control and supervision of their churches, just as they do in the white churches. Most of the direct work is carried on through colored clergymen, lay readers and women workers. Of the three classes of workers there are one hundred and nine, fifty-four and one hundred and twenty-nine, respectively, giving their entire time to the spiritual life of the Negro. For some time there has been a demand from the negro contingency of the church for a larger amount of self-control. A plan of "Suffragan Bishops," without right of succession, working under the control of the diocese, and also a plan of "Special Missionary Bishops," elected by the House of Bishops and subject to the diocesan Bishops, have both been suggested and seriously discussed. It seems quite evident that some definite plan will be adopted soon giving more self-direction to the Negro and still maintaining the integrity of the United Church.

The Presbyterian Church in the United States of America has two hundred and forty ministers—eight of whom are white—serving three hundred and eighty-one negro churches, in most cases partly or entirely self-supporting. They were able to report one thousand four hundred and twenty-two members added on examination during the year 1911, making a total membership of twenty-four thousand and forty-five (24,045).

The Congregational Church reports for 1910, one hundred and seventy-two churches in the South, probably one hundred and fifty of which are for Negroes. There are three hundred and five negro missionaries, ministers and teachers. In these churches there were ten thousand nine hundred and one (10,901) members, with seven hundred and ninety-nine additions. A glance at the report of the A. M. A., through which the church does its work, indicates that in most of these churches at least a part of the salary of the negro pastor is carried by the association.

The Presbyterian Church in the United States (Southern Church) has been carrying on through its Committee of Colored Evangelism an aggressive campaign, so that it can now report sixty-five churches, two thousand one hundred and ten members, and two hundred and four professions of faith. (Last report available, 1908.)

The Home Mission Board of the Southern Baptist Convention works in conjunction with the National Baptist Convention (colored), the two together supporting twenty-five missionaries in 1910, reporting two thousand four hundred and fifty-four (2,454) baptisms, three hundred and sixty-five Bible conferences, with an aggregate attendance of twenty-nine thousand eight hundred and eighty-eight preachers, and a total addition to the National Baptist Convention of five thousand seven hundred and eighty-two (5,782) members. If space permitted, one could go through the list of most, if not all, of the churches, showing that in practically every case something is being done. But enough has been said to show the method of work.

Sunday Schools.

Almost every local church, if not every one, has a Sunday school connected with it, and the number of scholars connected with the department frequently equals the number of church members. But not every Sunday school has connection with a church. In fact, some of the denominations are doing a splendid work through mission Sunday schools organized and taught by white people. In most cases these schools are pure missions and are connected with no negro church. Other churches have done much of this work, but perhaps the Southern Presbyterians have pushed it most vigorously. From the report of the Secretary of Colored Evangelism in this church we quote the following:

"Another feature of colored missions, which should be noticed here, is the effort to establish Sunday schools taught by white people. The number of these varies averaging about thirty. The most conspicuous success with such Sunday schools has been attained by those in Louisville, Memphis and Atlanta, though there are many smaller ones that have done much good. The largest mission of this kind in the entire South maintained by any white church, is that conducted by Rev. John Little at Louisville, Kentucky. He gives his untiring attention to two mission schools, including industrial classes for the poor and ignorant. Sixty (60) white teachers volunteer their aid, and the weekly attendance averages seven hundred and fifty. Recently other branches of the Presbyterian family have been invited to join in a co-operative effort to properly support this mission and erect suitable buildings. A commodious brick building has replaced the shack which has housed the Preston Street Mission so long."

Educational Work.

By far the most aggressive and widespread work among the Negroes is in the field of training. Here the need is so obvious that every church has taken a large share. The Congregational Church has two theological seminaries, three colleges, twenty-five secondary institutions, and thirty-eight ungraded and elementary schools. In these there are five hundred and seven teachers and officers, and thirteen thousand four hundred and forty-nine (13,449) students. The American Baptist Home Mission Society has an interest in, operates and aids twenty-six institutions in thirteen States, with permanent endowment of $320,000, property valued at $1,866,716, three hundred and fifty-three teachers, and eight thousand two hundred and sixty-five (8,265) students. Forty per cent of all these students are receiving instruction in industrial work. The Board of Missions for Freedmen of the Presbyterian Church in the United States of America has one university, five boarding schools for girls' schools, ninety-five academies, parochial and graded schools. On these schools they spent for the year ending May, 1911, $80,380.47. The Episcopal Church has a relationship to some eighty schools of all grades, but the American Church Institute, the educational board of the church, is now centering attention and effort on six—St. Paul's Normal and Industrial, Lawrenceville, Va.; St. Athanasius School, Brunswick, Ga.; St. Mark's School, Birmingham, Ala.; the Vicksburg School, Vicksburg, Miss.; the St. Augustine School, Raleigh, N. C., and the Bishop Payne Divinity School, Petersburg, Va. The Methodist Episcopal Church, South, spent on negro schools during

1911 $15,000. The Home Mission Board of the church is fostering Paine College, Augusta, Ga.; Lane College, Jackson, Tenn.; Miles Memorial College, Birmingham, Ala.; Texas College, Tyler, Tex.; Mississippi Industrial School, Holly Springs, Miss., etc. At one of these colleges—Paine—there are five Southern white college men and women as teachers. The Southern Presbyterians have Stillman Institute at Tuscaloosa, Ala., a school which is doing a noble work. The Christian Church, through its Woman's Board of Missions, has six industrial schools, mostly taught by colored teachers, save at their Southern Christian Institute near Edwards, Miss., in which all save two of the seventeen officers and teachers are white.

Industrial Training.

One most encouraging feature about all the missionary education is that it relates the students to every-day life. There has been a wonderful change in this regard in the last few years. Most of the schools started just after the war were anything but industrial in spirit, but in looking through the reports of all the leading mission boards, I find practically all of them are now stressing the training of the hand as well as the head. A very good illustration of this decided change can be found in the Penn School, St. Helena Island, S. C., which was established forty-nine years ago. In its early years it was purely classical, in so far as that was a possibility, for the term seems ridiculous when one knows the illiteracy of the people. On my recent visit to the school I found an industrial and trades building in process of construction. I visited carpenter shops and shoe shops, saw basketry work, sewing, cooking, farming, poultry raising, laundering, heard a lecture on nursing, saw the county teachers gathered there for counsel and instruction, and, about all, found an atmosphere of thrift and cleanliness which was wholesome and encouraging.

Of course, I do not mean that these schools are given over entirely to industrial work. Much attention is given, and rightfully, to other phases of training, but there is a much better balanced course of study than formerly.

Special Forms of Service.

There are some special forms of service undertaken by various churches which deserve mention here.

"The Woman's Home Missionary Society of the M. E. Church is undertaking a splendid work for the colored women of the South. Recognizing the fact that an intelligent, Christian home is one of the strongest bulwarks of a genuine civilization, that a nation rises no higher than the status of its women, and that, as the mothers are, so will the children be, they have undertaken to reach as many as possible of the future wives and mothers of the race with the means at their command so as to form nuclei of intelligent and Christian homes.

"We have fifteen of these industrial homes. They are not institutions, but veritable homes, where the golden chains of order, respect, interest, and love bind all into a common family.

"In all these industrial homes all branches of domestic economy are taught, such as domestic science, general housekeeping, laundry work, plain sewing, dressmaking, millinery, drafting, embroidery, drawn-work, crocheting, knitting, basketry, and all kinds of fancy work (of which they are very fond), as well as the proper conduct of a home, etiquette, ethics, morality and religion.[1] In this splen᷄ d work they spent during the last quadrennium $145 76.85."

᷄ ᶥe Methodist Episcopal Church, South, has two men (Southern and white) who are giving themselves to a thor-

---

[1] "Re o of Woman's Home Missionary Society of M. E. Church, 1908." p rt

oughly scientific investigation of the conditions and needs of the negro church, with a view to meeting these needs in so far as opportunity offers. Also there is a splendidly trained Southern young woman, Miss De Bardeleben, giving herself to the establishment of a deaconess' training department at Paine College. A letter just arrived from Miss De Bardeleben, after outlining the work done through the colored Sunday school teachers of the city, goes on to say: "Our Colored Civic Improvement League is a reality. We have about forty members, and are trying to get right away a trained nurse, to inspect, to advise and help with the sick in the poorer homes. I have the authority of the council leaders to build a cottage or workers' home here, and to begin in the house in a small way the training of young women for mission work." There is no greater need than just this type of trained social and religious worker, and one will watch with great interest the growth of this department.

The Presbyterians of the U. S. A. are starting a most interesting experiment in what might be called "farm housing" in Georgia. A large tract of land has been bought near Keysville, Ga., and is being rented in small plots to negro men with families. After the first year of rental, if the family proves industrious and willing to work, they can buy the plot on comparatively easy terms. The main idea of the scheme is to build up a group of model homes that are sanitary, attractive and comfortable. The Methodist Episcopal Church is putting special emphasis on Epworth League work among negro Methodists, having a special secretary set aside for supervising this work, who is able to report two thousand one hundred and fifty-four (2,154) colored chapters in 1911. Many other small undertakings are under way for the uplift of the Negro.

'A Comprehensive Study Needed.

The first impression one has, after a comprehensive review of the efforts of all churches, is that much unselfishness and genuine sacrifice have been poured out on the altar of this great cause. Surely men and women have shown their interest in plain, simple humanity, unadorned, not dressed up—just bare humanity.

Another of the most vivid impressions which one has after making a study of the reports of all the boards is that much of the work is done with inadequate information; there is much duplication, much overlapping of various denominations, much experimentation.

There is genuine need that a real study be made of this whole problem of missionary work and some comprehensive scheme worked out by which every church will have a full share, and yet there will be no duplication. The problem is entirely too large to be solved piecemeal, and it is entirely too pressing to allow any money or energy to be wasted. There are whole realms of endeavor now untouched by any church, and in other realms there is not a little overcrowding. If a commission of two or three scholarly men could be set aside for a careful study of the whole field of endeavor, thousands of dollars might be saved, hundreds more might be reached, and much future friction might be avoided. To make such a study would be a service to the entire country. Some college-trained men must do this work, and I am wondering what men will take this royal chance.

More Southern White Men Needed.

Another great need is that the finest flower of our young life in the South shall take hold of this big task. We are in the midst of it; we know this problem as no others can. These people are dying all about us; we have the message of life. How can we withhold it? Some of the choicest spirits of the South have already thrown themselves into this great battle. I challenge any Presbyterian to show me two more splendid men than Rev. John Little and his cousin, D. D. Little, both coming from homes of the old aristocracy in Alabama, now giving their lives to this great enterprise. Or who does not admire such a well-trained woman as Miss De Bardeleben, of the Southern Methodist Church? Or where can you find a more splendid type of a young educator than Jackson Davis, of Virginia? The hour has arrived for a great gift of Southern life to this colossal task. Within a week of this writing a letter has come from a choice college man, a senior in one of our best Southern colleges, saying he had been studying this problem and had deliberately decided to give his life to God in the uplift of the Negro. That is a momentous decision for a cultured Southern white man, but it is no bigger than God is asking.

The Southern Churches Must Awake.

No Southern man of any pride can read the scant reports of our Southern churches in their efforts to uplift the Negro without hanging his head in shame. Of course, we have been poor. Of course, we do not forget the heart-sickening scenes of reconstruction days. Of course, we have been misunderstood; *but if we are men we will forget the past in a mighty effort to redeem the present.*

What a call is this! Here at our very door is one of the greatest and most fertile mission fields the world knows. Here are nine million people, the vast majority of whom are living in poverty, ignorance, sin, and we, the Christian, cultured men of the South, stand idly by and watch these poor wretches wallow in their despair. What princely givers we have been! The Presbyterians last year gave an average of three postage stamps per member to this work. The Methodists averaged less than the price of a cheap soda water—just a five-cent one. The Southern

Baptist Convention has only been asking from its large membership $15,000 annually, or less than one cent per member, for this tremendous work. Men of the Southern churches, what do we mean? *Do we mean to say by our niggardly gifts that these people are hopeless and worthless in the sight of God? Do we mean to say that one cent per member is doing our share in evangelizing the whole nation? Do we mean to say that a dozen, or at most a few dozen choice men are all the Southern churches can muster to send out in this mighty warfare? Is it because we are poor or because we are prejudiced? Is it because we are ignorant of the need or indifferent to God's call? Or do we think God blundered when he created the Negro? Why do we not have a larger share in this work?*

Here is a great field ripe for the harvest. Here is a nation stretching out its hands to us. We know their life; we know their needs; we can help them if we will. *God pity the Southern Christians, the Southern churches and the Southern States if we do not awake to our responsibility in this hour of opportunity.* We need a vastly multiplied amount of money; we need a volume of deep, earnest, heart-searching, prayerful sympathy; we need an outpouring of the most splendidly endowed and gifted life. *What we have done in the past has been good; what we do in the future must be a thousand times better.*

CHAPTER VII

WHAT THE ASSOCIATIONS ARE DOING FOR
THE NEGRO

NOT THEY WHO SOAR

Not they who soar, but they who plod
Their rugged way, unhelped, to God
Are heroes; they who higher fare,
And, flying, fan the upper air,
Miss all the toil that hugs the sod.
'Tis they whose backs have felt the rod,
Whose feet have pressed the path unshod,
May smile upon defeated care,
    Not they who soar.

High up there are no thorns to prod,
Nor boulders lurking 'neath the clod
To turn the keenness of the share,
For flight is ever free and rare;
But heroes they the soil who've trod,
    Not they who soar!

          —Paul Laurence Dunbar.

CHAPTER VII

WHAT THE ASSOCIATIONS ARE NOW DOING FOR THE NEGRO

The first Colored Young Men's Christian Association in the world was organized in Washington, D. C., during the month of December, 1853. The second association was organized in Charleston, S. C., in April of the year 1866, and the third in New York City, February, 1867. The Charleston association has had a continuous existence since its organization, though at times it has been lamentably weak.

The first colored delegate who attended an international convention of Young Men's Christian Associations was E. V. C. Eato, who was present at the Montreal convention in 1867, representing the association work of New York City. At this convention, General W. T. Gregory, an ex-Confederate soldier of Fredericksburg, Va., in his report on the conditions of association work in that State, expressed a deep personal concern about the work for colored men. The following resolution was unanimously adopted by the convention:

"That the Committee on Associations of this convention be instructed to report such measures as, in their judgment, will best promote the formation of Young Men's Christian Associations among colored brethren throughout the United States and British provinces."

Mr. George A. Hall, of Washington, made extended tours throughout the South prior to the Indianapolis convention of 1870, at which convention he reported as follows:

"There is another branch of work in the South which it

may be proper that the convention specially consider in this connection—namely, the promotion of associations among colored men. There are already some six or eight of them. Of course, they are small and their resources are limited. It is believed, however, to be the plain duty of the associations represented in this convention to make ample provision for the prompt prosecution of the general work of visitation of all young men, without distinction of color, as soon as the season will permit."

Richmond Convention.

The International Convention of Young Men's Christian Associations for 1875 convened at Richmond, Va., and Major Joseph Hardie, of Selma, Ala., a prominent Southern Christian leader, was elected President. During one of the sessions a petition from the colored pastors of the city of Richmond was handed Major Hardie, in response to which he said:

"A number of requests for prayer for colored young men of this city have been handed in. There is a great work to be done among the colored men of the South. I place it upon your hearts and your consciences here to-night, and if you will carry it to the throne, God will bless the colored young men of this country, that they may be rescued from the inroads of disease and corruption and the many evils by which they are now surrounded. They are environed by temptations of which you and I know nothing—seductions, blandishments and difficulties beset their pathway. Nothing but the grace of God will enable them to stand and overcome these trials and walk in the paths of holiness."

At the next convention in 1876 at Toronto Major Hardie made another appeal urging work among colored young men by a Secretary of the International Committee.

First Secretaries.

After prayer was offered by Col. C. W. Loveless of Alabama, Dr. Stuart Robinson of Louisville, Ky., urged the necessity of immediate action. There and then seven hundred dollars were secured for the support of a secretary to work among colored men. The first Secretary of the Colored Associations was General George D. Johnston, an ex-Confederate soldier and a warm friend of the colored people. He spent a year traveling through the South, investigating conditions and needs, and reported at the Louisville convention in 1877. In this convention, held in the South, the Associations of North America deliberately voted to authorize the International Committee to continue definite work for colored young men. Representatives were there from three colored student associations—Howard in Washington, and Fisk and Walden in Nashville.

In December, 1879, Henry Edwards Brown, the founder of Talladega College, and also a graduate of Oberlin College, a man well known and respected both by white and black alike, became the Traveling Secretary of the International Committee in its work for colored men. It should be noted that almost exclusive emphasis was then placed on work among colored students in school and college and that emphasis was continued by Mr. Brown's successors so that to this day student associations outnumber others, in city and country. The first Colored Student Association was organized at Howard University, Washington, D. C., in 1869. The work has greatly prospered under the leadership of Messrs. W. A. Hunton and J. E. Moorland, who succeeded Mr. Brown as the Traveling Secretaries of the International Committee. The former, who is now Senior Secretary, began work in 1890, and the latter entered the service of the committee in 1898. At the present time the city section of the colored department reports 41 associations in existence, 60,554 members, 1,319 men serving on committees, 1,145 Sunday meetings for colored men, with a total attendance of 85,808, in which 480 men professed conversion, and 1,229 men enrolled in the Bible class.

The student associations report 91 organizations in schools having 9,178 young men enrolled, 3,775 of whom are members of the association. This department reports 1,051 men serving on committees, 1,369 enrolled in Bible class, and both city and student combined report buildings owned valued at $224,600.

Mr. Rosenwald's Offer.

The work of this department has had a great impetus during the past year through the generous offer of Mr. Julius Rosenwald, of Chicago. On the first day of January, 1911, at a meeting held for the purpose of launching a building campaign for the colored men of Chicago, Mr. Rosenwald offered to give $25,000 on condition a total amount of $100,000 was secured, and in his announcement of this gift stated that he would give a like $25,000 to any city in the United States which would, during the next succeeding five years, raise an additional $75,000 for a Colored Young Men's Christian Association building. Already the cities of Chicago, Philadelphia, Los Angeles, Atlanta, Washington and Indianapolis are erecting magnificent buildings for the housing of colored associations, taking advantage of Mr. Rosenwald's generous offer. It now seems quite likely that during these five years from ten to twenty of the leading Southern cities ought to be able to avail themselves of this offer.

Work for Women.

The Young Women's Christian Association sends a brief summary of the work for colored women, as follows:

"The colored associations aim as far as possible to carry on the four-fold work such as is found in most of our cities, although not every branch has been able to do this, partly on account of lack of equipment and funds and partly owing to the lack of a trained staff. All of them have a boarding home, an employment directory, Bible classes, a Sunday vesper service and a few educational classes. Some associations have developed the educational work so that it includes besides classes in elementary English, arithmetic and grammar, classes in domestic art and science planned to equip girls for wage-earning. The reading room and library, informal talks and entertainments are also features of the association. Junior work, too, has been somewhat developed among the younger girls, clubs and sewing and cooking classes being the most attractive features. . . . There are now in the United States ten colored associations. Four of these are branches of the central association and thus are affiliated with the national organization. . . . The colored associations are to be commended for their earnest efforts to co-operate with other organizations doing work for colored women. The Society for the Protection of Colored Women, which carries on a travelers' aid work in many cities, is glad to be able to send girls to the association home for a night or two, or until a respectable boarding place can be found for them. Valuable information has also been given to kinds of employment open in the city, and present vacancies. The associations work in harmony with other societies, such as the White Rose Society, and in all cases the field is so divided that there is no duplication or wasted effort."

The future policy of this movement is outlined as follows:

"1. Concentrate on the development of existing associations along the following lines:

"*a.* Securing of trained secretaries as local leaders.

(Provision has been made for the training of secretaries in our training centers.)

"*b.* Responsible committee work.

"*c·* Greater publicity.

"*d.* Systematic finance methods.

"*e.* Educational, physical, recreative and religious work.

"*f.* Enlarged employment and travelers' aid work.

"2· Organization for the present to be limited to those communities having a population of five thousand colored women, where conditions are most favorable for model associations.

"3· For other places where conditions do not warrant the establishment of an association, advise and suggest plans for study and investigation which may prepare for an association in the future.

"4· Preparation of letters and literature especially adapted to the needs of the colored field. Preparation of bibliography for those wishing to study the colored field. . . . A thoughtful study based on this outline will give anyone a working knowledge of specific conditions relating to colored women and their needs."

Need for This Work.

There cannot be any doubt about the need for such work as this which the associations undertake to do for and with the young men and women of the negro race. If the white college men and women need the inspiration and direction of these organizations, how much more do the colored students need them? These latter students have usually had less of home life, less of real religious instruction, less of training in leadership, and are, therefore, all the more dependent on outside influences for fostering their Christian activities.

It must be remembered, too, that the students in the

negro schools in the South, because of their small numbers, will have disproportionately larger power, and if the race is to become sober, moral and God-fearing, we must see to it that their leaders have proper moral and religious instruction. The three traveling secretaries of the Young Men's Christian Association, Messrs. Hunton, Tobias and Jones, all of them scholarly and sane representatives of the race, ought to insure aggressive policies for the religious life of the men students. The Young Women's Christian Associations are not apt to fall behind in this good work.

Conferences are now organized for the training of leaders in the student work. The first summer conference on the order of the Northfield conference for white students will be held in North Carolina this summer.

Needs for City Work.

Of all the Negroes, those living in *cities* are by *far* the most needy from the moral and physical standpoint. In most cases their housing is poor; ventilation is bad; usually the sanitation is atrocious; there is overcrowding, underfeeding, and lack of all beauty in the surroundings. Add to this the fact that even their schools and churches are often located in unsanitary, unsightly and noisy localities and the picture of need grows very dark. A modern Young Men's Christian Association building for Negroes, such as is now being erected in Atlanta, Chicago, Washington and other cities, ought to help solve some of the larger problems of the city negro life.

Example of a Cheerful Home.

What has just been said indicates one of the chief problems of negro progress—the negro home. It is all too frequently simply a sleeping loft, with none of the comforts or attractions which should tend to keep the boys and girls off the street. Many of the race have so long lived

under such handicaps that they scarcely realize that anything else is possible. What they need is an example of
real home-keeping. Not a tumbled-down old building aban-
doned by some white family, but a real building where
things can be kept clean, and where the simple, neat and
attractive furnishings can create a desire for better things
at home. The negro can have better if he wants it. He
can make good laboring wages; his services are always in
demand; but one main difficulty is to get him to want better
houses and more comforts. Many a mission school has
done its greatest work for the race, not through the recita-
tion room, but through the atmosphere of cleanliness and
simple comfort which surrounded and pervaded its buildings. A Young Men's or Young Women's Christian Association building ought to, in a larger sense, do this for a
whole city. Its real effect should be to create ideals and
stimulate ambition.

An Example of Christian Unity.

One of the most serious handicaps of moral and religious life among negroes lies in the factional spirit to be
found in the churches. Here denominational jealousies are
at the highest tension, and even two churches of the same
denomination may have the bitterest rivalry. Those who
look at the negro race from afar and suppose them one
united race in religion, politics and social life are very far
from being familiar with the facts. No principle of organization has yet been found in the negro church which is
able to bind large groups together and prevent church splits.
The Young Men's and Young Women's Christian Associations have had a great message to white Christendom on
this point. Men who work side by side for men during the
week are not apt to be wholly sectarian on Sunday. It does
not make them less churchmen, but it makes them more
tolerant and more Christian churchmen. This movement

established among the Negroes could not fail to have a similar result. Besides the sanity and straightforwardness of the associations would do much to overcome the over-prevalent emotionalism too frequently found in the negro churches. No greater boon could be given to the religious life of the race. Then there is a great need for real Bible study among these men and women. If this is needed among white men, why should it not be more needed among negro men, who have fewer teachers, less favorable home conditions and less training which fits them for a proper understanding of the Bible when read? In this field the associations have proven their unique ability.

Hygienic and Sanitary Training Needed.

The actual physical exercise of a gymnasium is not nearly so much needed by negro young people as it is by whites, because the former do not live such a sedentary life as do most of the latter in an ordinary city. But there is a tremendous need that there be someone in the community like a physical director who is open to all who want to know the laws of healthful living. We have long since passed the time when we consider the leading of class drills as the main business of the physical director of a city association. He or she is to be a community force making for better hygienic customs and better sanitary conditions. A gymnasium for a negro association would justify itself on the one score of baths alone. It is a well-known fact that comparatively few negro homes have bath tubs or even sufficient facilities or privacy for sponge baths. Neither are there any public facilities in most of our Southern cities. I have recently made an investigation of the conditions of recreation, amusement, public parks, bath houses, etc., open to Negroes in Southern cities. I have before me the facts from seventeen typical Southern cities, including such places as Richmond, Charleston, Raleigh, Columbia, S. C., Nash-

—12

ville, Knoxville, Atlanta, Augusta, Columbus, Ga., New Orleans, Baton Rouge, Little Rock, Dallas, Fort Worth, Austin, etc. Besides, I have the facts for a number of smaller places. In these investigation cards there is a question asked about baths open to negroes, and only one city of the entire list reports any such accommodations; that city is Columbus, Ga., the baths being found in the Young Men's Christian Association building. Columbus, by the way, is the only one of these cities having a modern Young Men's Christian Association building for colored men. In every one of the other cities the nearest approach to a bath house is a barber shop, usually dirty enough and entirely too expensive to encourage habitual cleanliness. This is not simply a health question, but a moral question as well. No man can be his best morally who does not have a chance to keep decently clean. It is not unlikely that public baths would pay for themselves through the reduction of criminal expenses.

An Athletic Center.

It is further true that our Southern cities do not furnish anything like adequate facilities for the social life of the Negro. There are very few public parks, only four of the above cities reporting such parks for Negroes, and two or three others having private amusement parks open to Negroes in the summer, but not run for the good of the community, but for the remuneration of the owner. It is a positive shame that in most of our Southern cities Negroes are not allowed to go to the white parks and no Negro parks are provided. If we want separation, then we ought at least to be fair-minded enough not to take all the parks there are and provide the Negroes none.

This is a most serious question. It means that the negro boy cannot play ball. It means he cannot have any real games, for no game worth the name can be played on the streets. Everyone who has studied just a little child psychology knows well that health and character call for play. It is as difficult to build child character without wholesome, clean sport as it is to make bricks without clay or straw. The negro child is no exception to this. This may be one reason why the communities around schools are almost always more quiet and orderly and the children better behaved because the school grounds are almost always used as a park and playground for the community.

Now, the Colored Young Men's Christian Association can help to meet this pressing need. It cannot take the place of public parks, but it can furnish indoor and outdoor play life to hundreds and hundreds of boys, just as the white association does for white boys. It is none too soon to start this work if we want to save the rising generation of boys.

A Social Center.

Neither is there anything in the way of a social center for the Negro during his leisure hours. No man can work all the time. Every man must have some leisure. These unoccupied hours are the most dangerous to the average Negro and by far the most costly to the community. It is during these hours that most of the quarrels and fights take place, and during this time also that most of the schemes for the worst crimes are conceived. As a matter of self-defense, we must take care of the leisure hours of these young people just as we must for any other class. Of the seventeen cities investigated, five report one or more theatres for Negroes, several allow them in the "peanut" gallery of the white theatres, and the other five report nothing of this kind of amusement. Eight of these cities have moving picture shows for negroes; nine have none. Of the nineteen picture shows reported in these eight cities, about half are reported as very low and degrading, having the cheapest and vilest vaudeville attachments. One investigator reports: "The principal places of amusement for the male population are the saloons, pool and billiard rooms." In one city "they are not allowed to attend the picture shows, and the one formerly run for them has closed up." Another investigator reports: "Negroes admitted into 'peanut' gallery in white theatres, but better class say they will not go unless for some special attraction, as they are put with the lowest class of whites." Another reports: "Picture shows with vaudeville attachment are rotten, attended by lowest types of all colors." Another investigator, this time a college president, whose thorough sociological training makes him a discriminating critic, writes as follows: "There have been several moving picture shows in ———— exclusively for Negroes. They have been on the vilest streets and have been attended largely by the worst element of Negroes, and from all I can learn the pictures have not been of the cleanest sort, to say the least." As certain as the recreation hour determines the character of a man or woman, so certain are we condemning thousands of these helpless people to a life of shame and crime by failing to provide for them or helping them to provide for themselves decent recreation.

The Colored Young Men's Christian Association of Columbus, Ga., helps to meet this situation, as do many other associations, by giving wholesome social life in its building. In its small auditorium once or twice a week it has high-grade moving pictures, which not only entertain, but instruct and elevate. Besides, in its parlors it has a piano, where the young men can indulge their musical abilities. There ought to be such a social center, both for men and women, in every Southern city.

Any organization which has shown its capacity to meet such needs as these, besides ministering to the deepest spiritual needs of the community, has a claim on the hearty support of every loyal Southerner.

County Associations Needed.

If, however, the students in the negro schools and the young people in the cities need associations, it may be maintained that the country Negro needs its work even more. There the humdrum of life eats like a canker into the fibre of ambition; the weary monotony tends to bring all existence down to a dead level of the commonplace. There are no new ideals; there is so little to stir ambition, so little to keep hope alive. The danger of the country is that all the more active young men and girls become restive and go away to the city. The one way to keep these better young people in the country is to make life there more virile.

In this connection one needs to refer to recreation again. Speaking of rural recreation, President Butterfield says:

"The closest observers of rural life are quite convinced that the recreations of the country, not only for children, but for young people and for adults as well, are grossly inadequate. Farmers themselves are, as a rule, apparently satisfied with the situation, and, as a matter of fact, if one should take a census of the recreations of the rural people, a long list could be named. But it would also appear that recreation on the whole is inadequate in amount, in variety and in quality; that the country people do not take sufficient time for play, and that such recreations as exist are unorganized and are not adapted to develop the best phases of character. There are notable exceptions to these general truths, and there are wide variations of conditions, but in general it is safe to say that rural life is lacking in recreation." [1]

This statement is almost too mild to apply to the negro community, for it can hardly be said that a long list of amusements for them could be named. In fact, I sent letters to more than two hundred workers among Negroes in

---

[1] "The Country Church and the Rural Problem," p. 42.

the rural districts and was able to get a list of only four types of amusements from them all—hunting and fishing, visiting shows and fairs, going to church, and going to town. This shows the terrible poverty of this side of the negro's life.

A Religious Demonstrator Needed.

In the chapter on the negro farmer, we have shown what marvelous economic results have come from the work of the United States farm demonstrator, who brings the farmer new ideas and up-to-date methods. In the chapter on rural schools we have shown similar splendid results coming into school life from the industrial supervisor, who is really an educational demonstrator. *What we need to complete the circle is a religious demonstrator in the person of a Young Men's and Young Women's Christian Association County Secretary.* This religious demonstrator would organize the play life of the community; would initiate and foster community meetings, which would create community spirit; would help to bring all the churches together in a real campaign for moral and religious uplift—in a word, he would become the moral, social and religious engineer of the community. Already the students of Pennsylvania State College have agreed to pay the salary of such a demonstrator for one county in the South, and a Hampton graduate, scientifically trained in agriculture, and hence sympathetic with the needs of the rural Negro, is now getting ready to open up the first field of service. Many other colleges ought to follow the lead of Pennsylvania State College and have their representative working in some of these local fields. I do not know of any place where a thousand dollars would do so much for the uplift of the negro race as if put into the work of a county secretary of the association in some of the darker counties.

Growing Interest Among White Men.

Perhaps the most important thing, however, which the association is doing for the Negro is not directly, but indirectly done. The difficulty for forty years has been to get an intelligent interest on the part of Southern white men in this problem. I have shown in the preceding chapter that the Southern man before the war was carrying on a much more aggressive campaign of betterment for the Negro than has ever been carried on since the war. In 1860 the Southern Methodists alone had 327 missionaries at work, most of them white men, and spent $86,000 in that year alone for the uplift of slaves. Now that the church has grown ten-fold, it is giving the paltry sum of $15,000 to a work for twice as many people. Every other Southern church is doing about the same. Southern white men have not been interested, and this has been the most difficult aspect of the whole problem. After my first volume for the study of negro life appeared, Dr. Booker T. Washington wrote me, saying that, in his judgment, the association was now attacking the most important and difficult phase of all the work—the interesting of white men in the problem.

Success of the Attempt.

No one with the least knowledge of the conditions hoped—even in the most sanguine mood—that we should find such a splendid response from the college men of the South as we have found. We had hoped that two thousand Southern college men might be secured for the study of the text-book[1] in small groups throughout the Southern colleges. What was our amazement to find four thousand studied it the first year? During the current year of 1911-1912 we already have nearly six thousand college men studying this same book. There were at the Agricultural and Mechanical College of Mississippi one hundred

---

[1] "Negro Life in the South," by the author.

and ninety-eight men enrolled in the study classes last year (1910-1911), and this year (1911-1912) five hundred and one have enrolled. In another State institution, where some of the students thought men would not study about the negro's conditions and needs, a canvass was made, offering the men a choice between a study of the foreigner and a study of the Negro, and at the close of the canvass it proved that ninety-six per cent of all the men had signed up to study the Negro. Similar success has been reported from many colleges.

A special reference liberary of seven volumes, entitled "Race Relationships in the South," has been bound in uniform bindings and is being put into most of the college and city association libraries, so that sane and scientific information is now available to all who are interested.

Social Service.

But not only are the educated men of the South willing to study this question; they are also beginning to put the knowledge into practice. A fine student in one college, after he had become interested in the study, brought together all the negro cooks, waiters, and janitors on the campus into a Civic Righteousness Club, where they discussed the problems of moral import to these men, basing it all on the study of the Bible. The white student was the leader. In another institution all the negro men working on the campus were organized into a straight Bible class, led by a white student. In one State university the Student Secretary of the association organized a civic club among the Negroes in the city where the university was located. The group, with seventy one initial members, met in a negro tailor shop and was led by the advanced white students. In another college the men are going out to the convict camp near by, teaching not only the Bible, but the simple rudiments of knowledge. They also hold a regular religious service for these men. In this work they have the most hearty support and co-operation of the warden, because he says it makes the convicts less sullen and more easily handled. In a great many colleges the white students have organized Sunday schools for negro children. In other places they have taught normal classes of the colored Sunday school leaders. Groups of white students have taken tours to leading negro schools and have invariably come away with a new conception of the Negro and his progress.

Investigations.

One of the most important needs of the times is **for** first-hand information. Men become interested when they go and see for themselves. One real tour of investigation is better than reading two books. Uniform investigation cards have been issued to guide students in their attempt to find the facts. Those who are going out have new eyes because of the study and because of the guidance of these cards. Dozens of Southern students are realizing the need for effort, because of such investigations, as they never could have realized them by study. One worker for boys in the South said recently that two years ago no college man would even consider working with negro boys, but now he could get more of the very choicest white students than he could possibly use.

A New Era.

This is the dawning of a new era. Those who know must of necessity be interested, and those who are interested will of necessity help. The need is appalling, but the response is becoming more and more enthusiastic. God is surely thrusting forth laborers into his harvest. It takes a little courage still for a white man to throw himself into this great conflict. There are still those who are not big enough to sympathize; they are only big enough to laugh.

Let no man who is afraid of his reputation; let no man who is seeking for honor; let no man who wants to win applause enter here. But if a man has a heart big enough to have it bleed because of the suffering of others; if his soul is sensitive to the bitter cry of hungry children, homeless women, struggling men; if he aspires, even in an humble way, to be in company with those heroic souls who have dared all for a great cause—then here is a place of service. In this service no man need be ashamed of his comrades, for here the little men will not dare. Here is Paul, the man who knew no race; here is Lee, who labored unselfishly for his own slaves; here is Jackson, than whom the Negro had no better friend; yea, here is Jesus Christ himself, with yearning heart, waiting to help this belated race. If we are big enough, let us aspire to this noble company, for of such friends no Southern man need be ashamed.

BIBLIOGRAPHY

Following the line of the bibliography of "Negro Life in the South," I here add a note about a few additional volumes which may help some to select those books most needed in this study. Each book has been carefully reviewed for this purpose. For further titles see bibliography in "Negro Life in the South."—W. D. W.

BRAITHWAITE, WILLIAM STANLEY—"Lyrics of Life and Love." Herbert B. Turner & Co., Boston. A series of poems of more that passing beauty by a Negro poet.

BROWN, WILLIAM GARRATT—"The Lower South in American History." The Macmillan Company. A true picture of the rise of the Old South and its early influence; just a little pessimistic in tone.

CUTLER, JAMES ELBERT—"Lynch Law." Longmans, Green & Co. A careful compilation of the facts of lynching and a statement of the causes and effects. It should be read by every Southern man.

DAVIS, DANIEL WEBSTER—"'Weh Down Souf." The Helman Taylor Company, Cleveland. Poems of the Old South of true beauty and sentiment.

ELLWOOD, CHARLES A.—"Sociology and Modern Social Problems." American Book Company. Contains a very illuminating chapter on the "Negro Problem."

JOHNSTON, SIR HARRY H.—"The Negro in the New World." The Macmillan Company. A compendium of facts about the Negro, very suggestive, and quite accurate on the whole, though a bit superficial as to Southern conditions.

MUNFORD, BEVERLY B.—"Virginia's Attitude Toward Slavery and Secession." One of the best statements yet written concerning the causes of the Civil War; not belligerent, but setting forth simple facts.

ODUM, HOWARD W.—"Social and Mental Traits of the Negro." Longman's Green & Co. A statement based on an extended investigation, but not altogether too fair-minded. It hardly lives up to its title.

PHILLIPS, ULRICH B.—"A Documentary History of American Industrial Society," Vols. I and II.   Arthur H. Clark Company, Cleveland.   Bringing together a great many of the old manuscripts bearing on plantation and frontier life; invaluable to the student who wishes to get back to first sources.

RILEY, B. F.—"The White Man's Burden."   Published by the author, Birmingham, Ala.   A very sane and sympathetic discussion of the negro question from a Southern man's standpoint.

STEPHENSON, GILBERT THOMAS—"Race Distinctions in American Law."   D. Appleton & Co   A clear, unbiased and helpful statement of just the distinction—and at times discriminations— made throughout the United States in the laws governing race relationships.

WASHINGTON, BOOKER T.—"The Story of the Negro," Vols I and II. Doubleday, Page & Co.   A history of the Negro, past and present, written in a most interesting and readable style.   It cannot fail to be of great service to all who want to know the negro as a race.

WASHINGTON, BOOKER T.—"My Larger Education."   Doubleday, Page & Co.   A continuation of the life story of the author, written in that easy conversational style which makes it very readable.   Like everything else Dr. Washington has written, it is fair-minded and will give ample returns for reading.

NOTE: The books in the foregoing list may be secured through ASSOCIATION PRESS, *124 East 28th Street, New York*

INDEX

www.ingramcontent.com/pod-product-compliance
Lightning Source LLC
Chambersburg PA
CBHW040135270326
41927CB00019B/3390